# FROM PRODIGAL TO PRODIGY

To order, call 256-759-7492
Visit us at www.spiritreign.org for information
on Spirit Reign Communications, The
Prodigal2Prodigy Project, and Families At The
Altar Ministries.

The author assumes full responsibility for the
accuracy of facts and quotations as cited in this
book.

Edited by Shirley Iheanacho
Cover and Interior Design by Daryl S.
Anderson Sr., Founder and CEO of Spirit Reign
Communications

Photographs by Aaron Lacy Photography
www.aaronlacy.com

Foreword by Eric Thomas
Michigan State University Founder of Advantage
Retention Initiative
PhD. candidate Educational Administration
Senior Consultant of International Urban
Educational Consultant
Senior Pastor Place of Change Ministries
www.etthehiphoppreacher.com

ISBN 978-0-9746231-3-9

# FROM PRODIGAL TO PRODIGY

## Jeremy J. Anderson

SPIRIT REIGN PUBLISHING
A Division of Spirit Reign Communications

B
A5473an

# Acknowledgements

## SPECIAL THANKS

Mrs. Shirley Iheanacho, Editor
Thank you for providing valuable input and for your tireless effort in helping to get this book finish. Your interest and belief in this project is greatly appreciated.

Patricia Simmonds
Thank you for your spiritual guidance, prayers and support throughout this journey.

Dr. James Doggette
Thank you for leadership and allowing me to serve and be active in church.

Dr. Jessie Wilson
Thank you for all your training and counsel on service and outreach.

Eric Thomas
Thank you for your continued years of support and encouragement.

Mackenzie Kambizi
Thank you for your friendship and for adopting me as your mentee.

Shannon & Shirley Austin
Thank you for your combined love and belief in me and my ministry.

PlayCousanS
Thank you all for your unconditional love, friendship and support of my new walk.

# *Dedication*

First and foremost, I want to dedicate this book to God, the Father, for being a perfect God; Jesus Christ for the plan of redemption; and the Holy Spirit for never leaving my side. Your amazing love overwhelms me.

## TO

My Mother, Tawanna Lynn Anderson, for being a mother who loved me unconditionally and always believed in me and encouraged me, regardless of the situation. Since birth you have always been my number one cheerleader!

To my Father, Pastor Daryl S. Anderson Sr., for being my Role-Model, Hero, Pastor, and Friend. Thank you for your guidance and encouragement during my spiritual journey. I appreciate your support with this project, sacrifice and vision for our family.

To my siblings, Ashley, Daryl, and David, for your love, jokes, tears, and support through the years.

To my late Grandmother, Patricia McCormick, for always believing in me.

To my late Great Grandmother, Mama Lola Hall Ard, for being a spiritual pillar for our family and for showing us how to love.

My Grandfather, Pastor Herbert Anderson, for the words of wisdom and encouragement.

My Grandfather, Jeffrey Johnson, for always having my back.

To my Grandmother, Dr. Katie A. Arnette, for all your love and support and for being the spiritual anchor in our family. Thank you for all the wise counsel you have given me through the years that has sparked my re-birth.

To my lovely wife, Traci Shanell Anderson. Honey, thank you for sticking by me through the hard times and for loving me unconditionally. Your prayers, love, and support have been instrumental to my growth as a person and in ministry. You have been by my side believing in me during this whole journey. Thank you for being my best friend!

# Contents

Acknowledgments ......................................................................5

Dedication ........................................................................ 7

Contents .............................................................................9

Prologue ..........................................................................11

Foreword .........................................................................13

Introduction ....................................................................17

Chapter 1 Church Boy ..............................................20

Chapter 2 Identity Crisis....................................................28

Chapter 3 The Real World ........................................36

Chapter 4 Welcome to the Club ............................... 42

Chapter 5 Last Call for Alcohol ...................................55

Chapter 6 The Ride of my Life ...................................61

Chapter 7 Life After Death ......................................70

Chapter 8 Rebuilding ...............................................79

Chapter 9 Exceedingly & Abundantly............................... 91

Chapter 10 GPS ........................................... 101

Final Word ................................................... 116

Notes .............................................................. 120

About the Author ...................................... 122

# Prologue

## FROM PRODIGAL 2 PRODIGY

### Prodigal

"Prodigal," as defined by the Merriam-Webster Dictionary, is *"a person who is extravagant, high-rolling, profligate, spendthrift, squandering, thriftless, unthrifty, wasteful, reckless."* There was a time in my life when I adopted many of these character traits. With so many temptations in the world beckoning for attention, you may find yourself taking on similar traits. A Prodigal lifestyle is not the type of lifestyle that God has in mind for His people.

### Prodigy

"Prodigy," according to the Merriam-Webster Dictionary, is "a person who is a miracle, a phenomenon, important, wonderful, sensational, extraordinary, marvelous, completes unusual accomplishments, or a highly talented child or youth." God expects us to be a peculiar people, and to do extraordinary things for His name's sake. It's never too late to claim the Prodigy in all of us through Christ Jesus!

# FOREWORD

There are tons of books in print that speak to transformation, books that reveal the *"real-life"* experiences of individuals and their road to redemption. "From Prodigal to Prodigy" is not just another book that chronicles the life of a misguided troubled youth; this book combines real originality with spiritual intellectual integrity.

*"From Prodigal to Prodigy"* is rich in both personal experience and biblical depth. The author gives us more than his mere experience, but provides the reader with spiritual nuggets and guidance needed to help his readers meet the transitional demands of life. Although the book was written about the author's life, it's not a book about him; it represents the challenges so many of our youth face and the decisions they will be forced to make.

Jeremy's path and mine crossed in 1997 during his Junior year in high school. Within just a few days of interacting with him in class, it was apparent God had a special calling on his life. But like most teenage males searching for their true identity and self-worth, he was torn. Jeremy was torn between following his passion for the performing arts and blazing a trail for Christ, and partaking in the pleasures of the world.

Like Solomon in Proverbs, chapter one, Jeremy cries out to both the churched and the un-churched. Having tasted the fruits of both worlds, he uses strong, colorful images to help the young reader lose focus of the fact that they are actually reading a book, and instead engages the reader in the content of the lesson.

20 "Out in the open wisdom calls aloud,
she raises her voice in the public square;
21 on top of the wall[d] she cries out,
at the city gate she makes her speech:
22 How long will you who are simple love your simpleways?
How long will mockers delight in mockery
and fools hate knowledge?
23 Repent at my rebuke!
Then I will pour out my thoughts to you,
I will make known to you my teachings.
24 But since you refuse to listen when I call
and no one pays attention when I stretch out my hand,
25 since you disregard all my advice
and do not accept my rebuke,
26 I in turn will laugh when disaster strikes you;
I will mock when calamity overtakes you—
27 when calamity overtakes you like a storm,
when disaster sweeps over you like a whirlwind,
when distress and trouble overwhelm you.
28 Then they will call to me but I will not answer;
they will look for me but will not find me,
29 since they hated knowledge

*and did not choose to fear the LORD.*
*30 Since they would not accept my advice*
*and spurned my rebuke,*
*31 they will eat the fruit of their ways*
*and be filled with the fruit of their schemes.*
*32 For the waywardness of the simple will kill them,*

*and the complacency of fools will destroy them;*
*33 but whoever listens to me will live in safety*
*and be at ease, without fear of harm."*

Proverbs Chapter 1:20-33

With each page, it is clear that this book is more than a "how to" for troubled youth. It is more than just a text that explains to troubled, often misunderstood youth how to find their true identity in Christ and their way to a prosperous and healthy life. For some, this book will be about a restored relationship with family members; for others a newfound relationship with Christ; and for others a self of respect and dignity. You will soon discover that this book is more about prevention than intervention.

One of the greatest challenges our youth face today is a disinterest in reading. Most of them entertain themselves with music, video games, and other forms of entertainment but more often than not, reading is a lost art. This is a major issue because it is through reading that the youth discover themselves and the world around them. It is my belief that *"Prodigal to Prodigy"* and books of this type will reintroduce reading to our Youth. Be prepared to start your transformation process!

**Eric Thomas**

*"And may you have the power to understand, as all God's people should, how wide, how long, how high, and how deep his love is. May you experience the love of Christ, though it is too great to understand fully. Then you will be made complete with all the fullness of life and power that comes from God."*
Ephesians 3:18-19 NLT

# INTRODUCTION

Early one Saturday morning I was awakened from a deep sleep by the prompting from the Holy Spirit to write a book. The thoughts in my head were so strong; I couldn't shake them from my mind. Mentally, I felt paralyzed and held captive by the Holy Spirit. I had never imagined myself writing a book. It is amazing that as I lay in bed the Lord began to give me chapter titles, the same titles outlined in this book. I was horrified by the mere thought of writing a book, so I asked the Lord, *"Who am I to write a book?"* As I continued to battle with my own discouraging thoughts, He continued to speak to me.

In the midst of questioning the power of God and focusing on my own thoughts of unworthiness, He made it plain to me what my assignment was. In 2011, I made a commitment that I would follow the direction of the Holy Spirit, and this book is the result of that decision. I am convinced that God wants me to find multiple avenues of sharing my testimony. It is my sincere prayer that He will use this book to increase your faith and trust in Him who is able to do the impossible!

The Purpose of this book is threefold:

- **To prove to you that you can never go beyond God's reach.**

You may ask me how I know. I invite you to read on further to find out. Too often we think we've done too much, or were too bad, or too nasty, or too filthy to come back to God, but that's a lie that Satan continues to perpetuate. This book is my story of how I lost my way in life; but through God's grace, I was brought back home. All of the tests that I have gone through have now turned into testimonies.

- **To help inspire and encourage others in their journey that there is hope.**

Who better to learn from than someone who has experienced it firsthand? In NO WAY am I glorifying anything that I've done nor am I proud of it. I would like to encourage parents to never stop praying for their children.

- **To share my story so that you may get a true glimpse of where I was and where God has brought me today.**

I urge you not to waste so much of your life like I did. We all belong to the Lord whether we believe it or not; He loves and cares for us more than we'll ever know. It is my deepest wish that you pray before reading this book and that you let the Holy Spirit work on your heart. Throughout this book, I will share many of my life experiences, which I hope will be a blessing and an inspiration to you and your journey with God. My goal is not to glorify the lifestyle that I lived, but to glorify the God who saved me from that deadly lifestyle. God wants to restore all of our lives as He did mine. The same God who saved a sinner like me, can and wants to do the same for you!

Many times we leave home and head down the path of a Prodigal Son or Daughter; but the good news is that your Father is at home waiting for you. Whether you're a teen, adult, prodigal, or pastor, I pray that this book will be a blessing to your soul. Being children of the Most High God, we are all Prodigies in our own way, destined for Greatness!

*God Bless You!*

# CHAPTER ONE

## CHURCH BOY

### *"Born and raised in the Church"*

I was born in 1980 in Dallas, Texas, and am the oldest of four siblings. Following me is my sister, Ashley, then my brothers: Daryl and David. We were all raised in a Christian home with a lot of love and support. Our family lived in Dallas until I was around the age of 10. From there we moved to New Jersey. While in New Jersey we lived in East Orange, and Plainfield. Around 1993, my father moved all six of us to Huntsville, Alabama. He wanted to attend Oakwood College (now Oakwood University) to pursue his call to ministry. Oh, let me not forget to tell you that my great-grandfather was a minister, my father, grandfather, and grandmother are all Ministers! That's right! I am what you can call a "P.K." Preacher's Kid, a *"Super P.K."* actually.

This chapter is entitled "Church Boy" because that's just what I was. I was raised in the church which played a huge role in my life, and I was happy to be there. I can remember being in the Pathfinders, getting excited about going to AYS, and singing in the choir. I must say my parents did a super job raising me in a God-fearing environment.

King Solomon, the wisest man that ever lived wrote these profound words: *"Train up a child in the way he should go: and when he is old, he will not depart from it."* Proverbs 22:6, KJV. I recall our worship time together as a family. On those evenings I would have to recite a Bible verse. I would scramble at the last minute to crack open the Bible looking for a short and memorable verse. Not only did I have to recite the verse, but most of the time my dad would ask me what the verse meant. This added a whole new element to worship for me because it became real and meaningful. My parents realized the importance of family worship as well as Christian education; and they made this a priority.

### *"Fitting In"*

Somehow, my parents enrolled all of us in Oakwood Academy/Elementary School. I'll never forget the first day of school. I had a fresh hair cut, freshly-pressed uniform, and I was ready to make my mark on the school. You know how it is; the new guy at school is popular for the first day just because he or she is new. After the first day of school you can remain popular or you can become lame; and my goal, of course, was to remain popular. Like every human, we naturally want to be accepted. After moving from Dallas to New Jersey and now in Alabama, it was important that I make a good first impression. I can tell you one thing; it didn't help my popularity vote any when my mom walked in the classroom taking pictures of me and asking me to pose with people I'd just met. Mothers, don't you just love them?

While in school I did my best to fit in. I was what you could call the class clown. I was the one who would do something crazy for the laughter and approval of my friends, only to experience the consequences of getting in trouble alone. I was such a terror that I was denied the opportunity to graduate with my 8th grade class. I guess the faculty and staff were scared I would do something crazy or extreme during the ceremony. My 8th grade teacher even told me I wasn't high school material. I thought, *"Come on now, maybe not college but high school?"* Why would I not make it in high school? I can remember half my class thought that I'd failed the 8th grade because of my absence during graduation. I couldn't wait for the next school year to start so I could show up and show out!

Here we are ready to take on Oakwood Academy. (When I say *"we"* I mean my friends and I.) While we were in Oakwood's middle school, we had our own little *"A-Team"* that would devise plans and pull off funny pranks within the school. You see, we all had big plans for high school. As a matter of fact, my plans were so large that they soon got me kicked out of Oakwood Academy which my parents worked so hard to pay for. I didn't see what the big fuss was about; I only devised a plan to cut off the school's electricity a couple of times. It's not like they couldn't reboot the power and computer systems in the school. The school's principal and staff felt that things within the school would run smoother without my personality and pranks; so I had no choice but to go to the public school in my area, J.O. Johnson High School.

While I was at Johnson for the second half of the school year, I probably went to class four times. It was there that I really hooked up with the wrong crowd. This was such a large school; it was easy for me to slip through the cracks. Unlike Oakwood, if I didn't come to class or school that day no one would come looking for you or call your home. I was like a monkey swinging free in the jungle and I could swing with the best of them. Needless to say, I completely failed the 9th grade due to lack of attendance. It was evident that the environment and area of the school were not nurturing for me, so my parents enrolled me at Huntsville High the following school year. There are consequences that come with every decision in life; trust me, I know.

We will all be held accountable for the choices we make, even at a young age. In order for me to catch back up with my correct grade I had to attend the Seldon Center which was a local after-school night school program. If I could change my hard-headed and rebellious ways while putting forth a little effort, I would one day catch up with my correct grade and graduate in time with my class. Although I didn't want anything to do with Huntsville High, I didn't have a choice. My parents made it clear that the only option for me was to get my act together. My dad's a pretty big guy I might add, and I was tired of those consequences that came with my rebellious and immature acts. While at this new school I felt like a fish out of water. I decided to take a different approach to fitting in.

This particular year I decided that instead of being the class clown I would get involved in some school activities. I knew how to make my peers laugh, but could I earn their respect? I soon joined the Army ROTC program. I got to wear those Army's uniforms every Tuesday, ride helicopters, and put up and take down the school flag every day. I didn't stop there either. I also joined the Sigma Psi Phi Fraternity; our colors were blue, silver and black. I remember one day I was chasing one of my girlfriends down the hallway and ran across the school's Track and field coach. He stopped me, of course, and after a brief discussion of my absence in class, we discussed my speed and he told me to meet him on the track after school. That afternoon I made the track team. I did all of this to try and find a positive way to fit in, and it worked.

### *"Ministry at a young age"*

Although my future was looking bright at Huntsville High School, my heart was still at Oakwood Academy. That year while I was away at Huntsville High, Oakwood Academy got a new Bible instructor by the name of Mason West. Mason came to Oakwood with a passion for youth and drama. He formed a Christian drama group called *"Actin Up,"* and all my friends were apart of it. I'll never forget the first play they performed. The play was called *"No Weapon,"* and it was life changing. The play was based on the song by Fred Hammond and the Bible verse found in Isaiah 54:17, *"No weapon that is formed against thee shall prosper; and every tongue that shall rise against thee in judgment thou shalt condemn. This is the heritage of the servants of the LORD, and their righteousness is of me, saith the LORD."*

I remember sitting there watching the play telling my mom that I needed to go back to the Academy, so that I could join *"Actin Up."* Her response to me was, *"Boy ain't no play gonna change my mind; you're doing just fine at Huntsville High."* The play was so powerful and the students (my friends) did such a great job performing that by the end of the play my mother said, *"I'll think about it."* What? Wait a minute! You'll think about it? You'll give me a chance? Needless to say, I got my act together and began to press the issue of me going back to Oakwood. It was important for me to press the issue of getting me back to the Academy with my friends; but I didn't want to get on my parents' nerves. I was intrigued at the fact that I could take my energy and sense of humor and use it in the form of a ministry. Don't get me wrong, I was a knuckle head, but I still loved the Lord.

That next year my dream came true, my parents, as well as the faculty and staff, allowed me to come back to school. My friends accepted me with open arms as well as the drama group *"Actin Up,"* and it felt good! Everyone had their part to play in the drama group except me. I was just glad to be back but I knew that one day my time would come. One week the drama group was traveling to another school to perform the play, and one of my friends who played the role of *"Peppy"* was unable to attend the trip. I thought this was my opportunity, and Mr. West gave me a shot! Once I passed the audition for the role I began to memorize my part and the rest was history. We traveled to several cities all around the U.S. performing the play *"No Weapon,"* and other skits.

In addition to the Christian drama group, I was a member of the *"Break the Cycle"* Conference. The founder of this movement was Eric Thomas. He was like a big brother/mentor to me and many of my friends. I remember he made us feel like serving Christ and doing the right thing for the right reasons was cool. B. T. C. was a non-profit organization dedicated to addressing the literacy and personal development needs of youth and young adults in low-income areas across our country. B. T. C. also advocates and helps with community-wide events that encourage young people to effectively express their feelings, wants, and desires while breaking free from cycles of negative behavior and hopelessness.

God instilled in me at an early age a passion for public speaking; and I made myself available to speak anywhere at any time.

From this point on, ministry was a part of my life. It was fun ministering to other youth using my God-given talents. I enjoyed ministry so much that near the end of my junior year of high school I decided to run for the Chaplain position for my Senior Class. Not only was I Chaplain in my Senior Class, but I was also Religious Vice President of the school. My senior year I took God's ministry to the next level. God instilled in me at an early age a passion for public speaking; and I made myself available to speak anywhere at any time.

I remember the first time I preached at a church; it is still vivid in my memory. It was at Madison Mission SDA Church. The engagement was Academy Day, and it was the custom for the Religious vice president of the school to deliver the message at the local church that day. That was me! This was a big day for my family. My grandma Katie came in town to hear me speak, and even bought me a new suit to wear. It was black with silver pin stripes. I wore a white shirt and a silver tie to match. This was such a monumental day for me and my family. I preached on the message of love, the love that God has for us. I even wrote the appeal song, and when the appeal time came, the Holy Spirit showed up strong!

You see Madison Mission was a new church at the time and the majority of the members were college students; so most of the people who came up for the appeal were in high school or college. The message I delivered that day was tailor-made for my peers. That was the first time I knew I was truly used by the Holy Spirit. I know it wasn't me that got all those young people to come down for the appeal in tears. The feeling was unreal, like an out-of-body experience! Afterwards I was beyond tired. I didn't know then, but I now know that's what happens when the Spirit comes inside of you and takes complete control. Pastor Doggette, senior pastor of Madison Mission, and others, told my dad after the sermon that I was called for ministry. I think subconsciously that the more I heard this, the more I ran.

Look at me now! Just a few years ago I couldn't even graduate with my 8th grade class. The following year I got kicked out of a Christian academy; then I failed the 9th grade; and now I'm standing before hundreds preaching the gospel of Jesus Christ and His love for us. I was showing characteristics of a child prodigy, so I thought. I believe one thing that kept me grounded to the Lord was my involvement in ministry. I had such a hard time when I was younger because I was trying to seek the approval of my peers as opposed to the approval of God. Oh, how often do we do that; we are more concern what our siblings, friends, coworkers, neighbors think that we put God on the back burner; and His opinion is the only one that really matters.

# CHAPTER TWO

## IDENTITY CRISIS

### *"My College Experiences"*

I successfully graduated from Oakwood Academy in 1999. Now that high school is behind me, I am now on the way to the College that both of my parents were graduates of. With my father now in the ministry, my family moved to North Carolina. I went to North Carolina with them for about two months during the summer until school started for me back in Huntsville. I couldn't wait to get back and experience my freshmen year at Oakwood College.

I entitled this chapter *"Identity Crisis"* because that is just what I was about to go through. My soon-to-be-college experience would be quite an interesting one. Watch closely how the enemy can get you off track and place you on another one. Sometimes with our disobedience, we are delaying the things that God has in store for us. Disobedience to God's will equals delayed achievements. Please rest assured though that God is in control of everything. *"And we know that in all things God works for the good of those who love Him, who have been called according to his purpose."* Romans 8:2, 8, NIV.

My freshman year of college was a little different from

28

the average freshman's experience. You're talking to a guy who practically went to the college his senior year in high school. You see our high school was on the same campus as the college so all of the liberties that the average college student had, I experienced and more because both of my parents worked for the school. One of my close friends and I even took college girls to our high school banquet (which was like our prom). That's right, still in high school dating college girls. I even went to the colleges banquet my senior year in high school with a college senior. Yeah! I thought I was pretty smooth back then.

As a freshman at Oakwood I knew the who's who on campus, and I made it my goal to be on that list. College was a new experience in a way for me and my friends. Although we were familiar with the campus and students, while in high school, we still lived at home with our families. Now, we're adding the dorm life to our college experience which was one to remember. My freshman year I made some close bonds with friends both guys and girls who are still dear to my heart today.

### "Spiritually Dead"

During my freshman year I was still involved in *"Actin Up"* the drama group. We performed plays and skits in college and my spiritual life was somewhat still in place. I was still going to church faithfully, and I didn't miss an AYS service. Church was still an important part of my life, but that slowly but surely began to dwindle. One thing I've learned about the enemy, Satan is the master deceiver. You can never say never with him. There are many things I said I would never do; and now as I sit back and look at what I've gone through, everything that I said I'd never do, I did, but on a larger level.

I know
that one of
my biggest
downfalls
in my
spiritual
growth
was my
lack of
ministry.

I know that one of my biggest downfalls in my spiritual growth was my lack of ministry. The drama group on campus only lasted a year, and I began to see the effects of it ending. *"But do you not know, O foolish man, that faith without works is dead?"* James 2:20, NKJV. I didn't realize ministry wasn't only making a difference in other people's lives, but it was making ALL the difference in my life. Slowly I began to lose myself as well as my identity to worldly ways. I began to get caught up in the world and all it had to offer. You see my friends and I were known on campus. My sophomore year in college I had a convertible car, part-time job, money in my pocket, women, etc. Life around those times was good! I began to get consumed with the world and all its glamour. I slowly began to do all of the things I said I would never do, like going to night clubs and drinking alcohol.

I remember the first time I was drunk. It was at a surprise birthday party my friend threw for me. Everyone was there, and I was in full effect! You see, there was this special birthday punch made just for me. It transformed me into a party animal. That night I remember being wild and untamed. After the police shut the party down, in my drunken nature, I jumped in my car, dropped the top to my car and told the crowd to follow me to the next location. Luckily, one of my best friends grabbed my keys from me and stated that he would drive me since I was drunk. My response to this kind gesture was, *"It's your fault I'm drunk, but OK."* Little did he know I had a spare key, and he was beyond shocked to see me pull up the second time blasting my music in my convertible! He asked *"How did you start the car?"* Laughing I said, *"With the key fool!"* He said, *"But I took your keys."* With a smirk I said, *"But not my spare."*

Laughing, he demanded those keys as well, and I had enough sense to let him drive me to the next location so that we could continue to party.

That night at my party was my first true encounter with alcohol. The next day everyone told me how much fun I was, and how they had a blast at my party. I was the life of the party. Sometimes in life you'll hear laughter, and you'll think people are laughing with you, only to find out that they are laughing at you; and you're not laughing. Now, at the time I didn't realize how dumb I looked drunk; I just realized how alcohol made me feel. I began to find comfort and pleasure in drinking. At the time it seemed fun and similar to an out-of-body experience. I thought I could just drink and hang out with my friends and have a good time; but I was wrong! Unfortunately, it got to the point where I couldn't have a good time without drinking. Every weekend, and eventually every day, alcohol was involved. For me and my friends this was a way of life. My hobby with alcohol soon became my habit! I remember in high school saying I would never drink; and now here I was, an alcoholic.

After sometime I took on the title of *"Angry Man,"* I could be two totally different people once I was drunk. I could be your best friend bringing you drinks just enjoying life, or I could be the one that if you made me angry, I would flip out. I recall leaving the bowling alley with some friend one night and having an altercation with the manager of the Bowling Alley. As I staggered to the counter to pay for my game, I couldn't find my wallet. While searching some more and talking to my friend, the guy behind the counter says, This guy is drunk and broke. *"Wine is a mocker, strong drink is raging: and whosoever is deceived thereby is not wise."* Proverbs 20:1, KJV.

Many times in life we find ourselves traveling down the wrong side of the road.

Instantly anger and hate raged within my body. Without thinking, I grabbed the manager of the bowling alley by his collar, pulled him over the counter, and introduced my fist to his face. Immediately my friends pulled me off of him, and we instantly fled the scene. This story only gets worse. While laughing at what just happened, I jumped in my car and drove on the highway, going the wrong way! I was literally going down the wrong side of the highway, and didn't realize it until I saw headlights coming my way. That night in spite of my prodigal and reckless ways, God spared my life.

Many times in life we find ourselves traveling down the wrong side of the road. Not sure how we got there and not sure how to turn around, we feel lost and confused. *"Be sober, be vigilant; because your adversary the devil, as a roaring lion, walketh about, seeking whom he may devour."* 1 Peter 5:8, KJV. I don't know how I got turned around and back on the right side of the highway, but I thank God for friends who weren't as drunk as I was.

### *"Pistol Play"*

My life was completely out of control! There were countless times when I woke up with women I didn't know, or woke up in my car on the side of the road, or with damage to my vehicle. There are countless times when I awoke the next morning from my drunken stupor asking what happened the night before? Reality really set in one day when I found myself staring down the barrel of an Uzi machine gun. This took place in broad day light as I stood in front of three guys, two of them had guns. I got into an altercation with one of the biggest dope dealers in Huntsville, and he was one squeeze of the trigger of this semi

32

automatic weapon from taking my life. So many times my life was threatened, and I'm here to tell you that not everyone is as fortunate as I was. God spared my life countless time so that I could warn you from going down that same wasteful and deadly path. After this violent and hostile standoff in broad day light, he and his crew eventually fled in their car. As they left the scene, they promised me that it wasn't over!

Life for me at that moment changed. Instead of being scared straight, or realizing the danger my reckless lifestyle had me in, this situation actually pushed me closer to the world. I was angry and enraged at what just took place. I went and told my boys what happened, and we went in search of these guys. We looked all around the city and were unable to find this guy and friends who threatened me and my life. After a while I realized I needed to put the bottle down and protect myself. I went to a local guns shop in Huntsville and bought myself a gun. My first gun was a chrome-plated .45. She was so pretty that one of my friends teased me saying that it was too shiny and pretty to do anything with it. He was right; I wasn't a killer nor did I have those characteristics. I just felt I needed to protect myself. Better him than me were my thoughts. I vowed to never be caught without protection. I soon bought two more pistols; this time they were black 9mm, something a little more conspicuous. One of my pistols stayed in my car at all times; the others were placed around the house.

In court a few months later, I ran into the same person who threatened to take my life. He was in the hallway of the court house wearing an orange jump suit with chains on his hands and feet, with a chain that connected them both. He looked as ruthless there in the hall of the courthouse as he did out on the streets. He was in court that day facing some serious federal time. He was facing life in prison and had nothing to live for. He could have easily pulled that trigger, and I would have been just another person who fell victim to his gun. Thankfully, God spared me. That wouldn't be the last time I had guns waved at me or bullets shot at me. I'm sure the reckless life I was living kept my guardian angel busy; and I didn't realize how far off course I'd gotten. That's what happens when you travel down the wrong road; you lose track of yourself, and you get lost. The longer your heading in the wrong direction, the worse your situation gets.

Here I am in Huntsville, Alabama, a functioning alcoholic, carrying a gun around with me everywhere, paranoid, and frustrated. The devil has a way of manipulating your mind. I started to take on certain characteristics. I was going through an Identity crisis! I wanted to make sure everyone knew I had a street side to my personality. Countless times I was caught up in foolish and violent acts. The thought of having a pistol in the car if things got out of hand and the encouragement of my liquor only made things worse. I was totally immune to consequences. I even kept a gun in my dorm room while in College. Foolish me! I had no respect for my elders, school, or authority.

Some of my friends and I came upon a large amount of weed. We smoked and sold it daily. I really liked smoking weed and my liking for it soon turned into a love for it and how it made me feel. Like alcohol, this love affair soon turned into an addiction, an addiction that I didn't want to quit. Weed calmed me down and kept me cool. I loved everything about the process of smoking, from breaking the weed down, to splitting the shell, to rolling the perfect blunt. I loved to smoke it, and passed the pleasure to my friends so that we could get high together. There was an art to smoking, and it was one that my friends and I mastered. Weed would take complete control over my body; and needless to say, my appetite. Little did I know this affair with drugs would be one that would have a strong hold over my life for many years to come.

We are
to be a
peculiar
people,
not the
kind that
conforms
to the
world.

FROM PRODIGAL TO PRODIGY

# CHAPTER 3

## THE REAL WORLD

### *"My Experiences after College"*

I thought after much practice I was the master of weed and alcohol. I was able to still handle my business in school while practicing my habits outside of class. I finally graduated in December 2004 from college. This was a much-needed accomplishment. You see, I changed my major from communications, what I was studying my junior year in college, to social work. I know that sounds crazy! This wild guy who smokes, drinks, and carries a gun everywhere he goes is about to be a social worker? Don't get me wrong, I really thought I was a good guy who wanted to make a difference. This is not the type of lifestyle that God wants for His people. We are to be a peculiar people, not the kind that conforms to the world. You can never tell a book by its cover. You think you know someone, but you may have no idea who the real person is.

After graduation I went on to pursue my dreams of getting my master's in social work, a MSW degree from Alabama A&M University. After completing the first year of the program, I had to drop out due to my lack of commitment and schedule. You see, I was managing a restaurant during the day and taking classes at night. The second part in completing the MSW program would be for me to work full time in a social work agency during the day. This would be fine, but instead of getting paid for my work, I'd be getting a grade. This wasn't going to work for me; so I told myself that I would come back and finish the MSW program later.

The restaurant soon closed due to Hurricane Katrina or at least that's what the owner of the restaurant said. So I began to apply for jobs, and I was ready to take the corporate world by storm. In spite of my reckless lifestyle, I knew how to talk and be professional while handling business. I was soon contacted by a company that was one of the largest car rental companies in the world; and they wanted me.

I was now a part of the corporate world. The corporate world was a world full of suits and ties, brief cases and cuff links, business meetings, and lunch appointments. I was really enjoying this new business lifestyle. I worked there for a total of two years, and gave the company my all. I even began to get promoted at several branches in the Huntsville/Madison area. I ended up managing several locations and was making some pretty good money for myself. My salary was not only paying my bills but also funding my habits of expensive top-shelf alcohol and all the weed my city had to offer.

Every Friday night I was at a bar somewhere in the city surrounded by my friends and women, drinking and being merry. I had money in my pocket and an appetite for beautiful women. I would flash money around and brag on my finances. I'd have a stack (thousand dollars) in my pocket nightly living a lavished and flashy life. While out and about in the city, I would specifically target older women. I had a fetish for women older

I was totally consumed and driven by money, flash, fame, and cars.

than myself. By now I was about 24 and if you were a successful, beautiful woman at least 30 years old, I was interested. There was something addictive about conquering successful older women. I was truly evolving into a Prodigal person in a foreign land. I would spend as much or more money on my drug, alcohol, and women habits than I would on my bills.

I was totally consumed and driven by money, flash, fame, and cars. You see as a manager at a car rental company I could get rentals to drive for free or a large discount; so every day I stayed in a brand new car. One week it might be a Chrysler 300, the next it may be the big Cadillac DTS; then the following week I might change it to a Chevy Suburban or Tahoe. If the weekend was special, I would grab a couple of Mercedes Benzes for me and my friends to enjoy for the weekend.

During this time in my life Satan really had a hold of my mind and thinking process. Not only did my close friends reap the benefits of my management position in the company, but I was also able to make some good side money as well. Every drug dealer needs a good vehicle to use. It's important in their profession to remain as anonymous as possible; that's where I came in. When the dope/drug dealers which we called *"d-boys"* would walk in my branch to rent a car, I could spot them off instantly. In search for their business, I would pull the local d-boys aside and tell them that I have exactly what they need. After a brief conversation, they would know that I was hip to the dope game, (drug game) and I would earn their trust and money.

You see, most drug dealers don't qualify to rent cars. To meet car rental requirements, there are several things you must have. A valid driver's license, a major credit card, proof of residency, and employment information, etc. Since none of them could qualify to rent a car, they had no choice but to go through me. This was always for a price, of course. To set the deal up, I would work the system and find a way to get them in a car that fitted their need. They were normally easy to please.

I supplied just about half of the d-boys in the city. This went on for about a year. There weren't too many people involved in the drug game that I didn't know. I began to build some good relationships with the d-boys around the city. Whether you needed a good car for the weekend or a whole week, I was the man to see. My sales and commission went through the roof, and my pockets daily were getting fatter.

The way I was working the system was risky, illegal, and unethical in every way. My reckless acts at work were a reflection of my reckless lifestyle outside the work place. I was so controlled and consumed with my addiction to marijuana that I would leave from work on my lunch break, go home and smoke a blunt, brush my teeth, put some Visine in my eyes, spray on cologne, and head back to work to finish the day. This was an everyday habit. I couldn't operate without weed. If my clients who I illegally put in vehicles didn't pay with cash they would pay with product. Good drugs for a car for the weekend; I'd take that deal some days especially if I were running low with my personal stash. The way I was operating at work at the time, I thought was genius, but it was actually pathetic. Here I am risking my career, a career I much needed for a couple hundred bucks a day. I was driven by the idea of having more money. *"For the love of money is the root of all evil: which while some coveted after, they have erred from the faith, and pierced themselves through with many sorrows."* 1 Timothy 6:10, KJV.

I began
to master
the role
of a split
identity.

FROM PRODIGAL TO PRODIGY

My mind was cloudy with the impurities of weed, the chase for money, and the love for alcohol. I began to master the role of a split identity. Life for me should have changed some by being a part of the corporate world. I didn't want to totally change my thuggish, reckless ways, so I adapted. I turned in to a chameleon. From 9 a.m. to 6 p.m., I was in a suit and tie handling business with the best of them. When I was off work, no later than a half hour from being home, I'd be smoking a cigarette, drinking a beer, while rolling a blunt. This was my lifestyle. When I would see these dealers on the streets, and they would see me in my regular clothes, they would look at me in disbelief. It would blow their minds for them to see me dressed down like them at night but in a suit during the day.

### *"My Fall for Women"*

There was now a new addition to my addiction. Beyond the want and need for weed, the drive for money, and the addiction to alcohol, I was now plagued with the lust for women. I found fulfillment in the pleasure of different women. Out of all of my addictions, this by far was the greatest because before weed, money or alcohol possessed my life, there was my deep lust for women. Weed, I couldn't sleep without it. Alcohol, it tasted so sweet to me. Money, I had to have more and more of it. Women and my lust for them conquered me. I enjoyed the chase of being with a new woman every weekend. In my teen years, I vowed to stay a virgin until I was married; now I was sleeping with more women than I could remember.

My mind was totally perverted! I enjoyed that challenge of having someone new in my bed. Key word here is *"new"*. It could be a new hair style, new perfume scent, new body

40

shape, etc. I just loved beautiful women and everything about them. My goal was to experience every shape, every body style, every nationality. I didn't care if she was Black, White, Korean, Hispanic, Indian, or Latino. She could be a fine ghetto chic or a 40-year-old corporate executive. She could have green eyes, brown eyes, black eyes, long hair, short hair, wavy hair, or the natural look. I didn't care if she was tall, short, skinny or thick; it didn't matter to me. What mattered to me was that I had them all, and this really scared me.

I didn't realize at the time how my addiction to women had such strong hold on me. I felt I would never get married. The way women would give their bodies to me shocked me. Here I am saying whatever I could say to get between their legs. I was what some would call a dog; and I didn't care.

If you're a man reading this book, you must understand the power that you have. God put us here to have dominion over the land. We must not take advantage of our responsibility and power. God gave us dominion over everything, and he expects us to take care of His land and all of His creations, especially the woman. God also put us here to be the leaders. If you're a woman reading this book, you must realize how special and precious you are to God and this world. Hold on to your virtue. I was not sane spiritually or mentally. I was emotionally disconnected. *"Who can find a virtuous woman? For her price is far above rubies."* Proverbs 31:10, KJV. To my dear sisters, find your virtue. Claim the glory that God has put within you. I want to personally apologize to every woman that I have taken advantage of !

*"A woman's heart should be so hidden in God that a man has to seek Him just to find her."* — Maya Angelou

# CHAPTER 4

## WELCOME TO THE CLUB

### *"My Introduction to the Club Lifestyle"*

There were many perks that came with my role of being a manager. I was in somewhat of a position of power; and I showed that power at every opportunity I could. One day while working in the office, a well-dressed gentleman came into the branch to try to rent a car. His credit card was being declined, so he sat in my lobby. After a while I noticed that he was still sitting in my lobby for over a half-hour. I asked one of my workers who assisted him what was the problem, and why was he still here? My employee informed me that his credit card was declined.

The gentleman in my lobby was well dressed so I inquired what he did for a living, and my worker told me that he was a club owner of a new night club in town. This set off my money making radar, and my antennas went up. I was intrigued to meet the well-dressed club owner and to see how I could help him. I will call the club owner *"Mr. B."* After a detailed discussion with him I felt comfortable to place him in his vehicle of choice.

My plan was to build a relationship with this guy so that I could use him to my advantage. After constant contact with Mr.

B, he begins to tell me how his new venue was struggling. He wasn't getting the crowd in the club like he expected; so I told him I would stop by his place later that week and checkout his venue. When I walked in I was impressed. Nice floors, leather booths, nice big dance floor, large bar, etc. The ambiance of the club was captivating; and I had a plan to get the place filled.

My friends and I were known for having large and crazy house parties. Whenever one of our birthdays would come around, we would throw a big birthday party; and mine was around the corner. I went to Mr. B and asked him how he felt about having his club filled on a Saturday night? He said that would be nice but how did we plan on doing this. I told him that it was my birthday, and I planned to throw my Birthday Bash there at his club, and it wouldn't cost him anything. I told him he could even charge most of my guests at the door. He hesitated but reluctantly agreed. I assured him that he would have a packed house. Between me and my friends we knew most of the city. He asked me what school I went to and when I told him Oakwood, he laughed and said, *"Isn't that a Christian school?"* I laughed and said, *"Yes, but we can party with the best of them."* This was not the kind of representation we are to have. The Bible says in Matthew 5:13 that we are to be *"the salt of the earth."* At this point in my life I went out of my way to show the world that I was just like them.

Once we agreed on the details of the party, I instantly spread the word. This would be the party of all Parties! I immediately picked up my phone and called and texted all of my closest friends. My close friends came in from Texas, Tennessee, and Georgia for this shindig. I told everyone to dress up because I didn't want this to be the average party, and I had a certain

I remember when I was young saying that I would never go to a night club, and now here I was running and promoting one.

corporate element ego; so it was agreed that we would keep the grown and sexy atmosphere. *"Grown & Sexy"* is club talk translated to "dress up for the occasion like an adult."

That night, as we promised, was a packed house. We ordered a few cases of champagne, and my closest friends and I were in VIP having the time of our lives. After the party, Mr. B was happy how the night turned out and at the size of the crowd. I saw this as an opportunity to make some serious money. My group of friends and I sat down and had a long talk about doing this full time. It was agreed that we would pursue this opportunity. So two of my friends and I put our money together and started an entertainment company.

We went back to Mr. B with a proposal for weekly parties; after some negotiation; he agreed, and we signed a contract. You see, Satan will give you opportunities the same way God will. Believe that the enemy's opportunities are never in your best interest. What glitters isn't always gold. So here was the Birth of our entertainment company! I remember when I was young saying that I would never go to a night club, and now here I was running and promoting one.

My friends and I single handedly transformed the city of Huntsville and its night life. You see, we added a much-needed element to the club scene. Every other club in the city was a regular club where you could wear sneakers and baggy jeans; but at our club in order to step foot in the door, you had to dress up. This had been done before every other month, maybe but never on a consistent basis. I'm talking tailor-made suits, stilettos, the little black dress ladies like to wear, hard bottom shoes, blazers, etc.

The city was extremely receptive to our style of party.

You only found this type of night life in major cities; and we were proud to bring it to ours. Adults from 25 and up finally had a place to party and have a good time without worrying about someone shooting in the parking lot, or fighting in the club. This became a place for the sophisticated and classy to socialize. It fit perfectly with Mr. B's vision of his night club. Fortunately for him, we were the ones to make it happen at a level of consistency that hadn't been done before.

Here I am an Oakwood College graduate, with a career and an entertainment company on the side. My friends and I were known around the city on another level. When you're running and operating the newest and hottest club in town, you automatically make a lot of friends as well as enemies. The style that we portrayed in the club was unheard of in the city; and it became contagious. I had one of my business partners on the microphone along with the DJ keeping the crowd entertained, while my other partner is showing the city how to wear a 3-piece suite while maneuvering through the club. I would sit back and greet our guests, shake hands with the *"who's who"* in the city, and keep the ladies entertained. We wouldn't just drink top shelf liquor *"expensive alcohol,"* we would drink champagne. Every party was a reason to celebrate. At this time my mind was so cloudy that I couldn't see what Satan was doing. You see Satan will give you what I call "false success". This temporary success is when he allows you to gain certain things, but you're really acting like a puppet for him!

### *"Greed & Hate"*

Every party for us was a celebration. We were surrounded by women; having a blast with our friends, drinking good in

VIP, smoking what we wanted, and the whole time we were making Money! The love in the city began to grow at a rapid pace, and the envy that Mr. B had for us began to grow as well. Yes, Mr. B was making money, but he didn't like the attention we were getting and the fact that people thought my friends and I were the club owners. We later saw firsthand how grimy and dirty this club business can be. There is a lot of crime, drugs, and violence involved in the club business; and in order to stay on top, we had to show that we were willing to do whatever it took to stay in the game.

The owner of the club, our business partner, thought now that his venue was the hottest club in the city; he didn't need us to promote or manage his place. After all we did for his business he didn't want to re-sign the contract! If we did decide to renew our contract, he wanted to give us a much lower percentage of the revenue. This was an insult; so we decided not to re-sign. We knew that the people in the city would follow us wherever we went. It is true that Mr. B's club was nice and all, but the city fell in love with our style of party, not with his club; so we parted ways. Through my connections at my job, I also built a great relationship with another guy who owned another club in the city. This guy loved me like a son. I called him *"Uncle Drew."* Whenever we would stop by his club, Uncle Drew would send a waitress to our table with a free bottle of liquor; he made it known that we always had a home at his club. Even though his club had a more urban feel, this was something to consider.

After parting from doing business with Mr. B, we decided to take Uncle Drew up on his offer. You see while we were in business at Mr. B's club, we took business from every other club in the city, and their doors always shut early on Saturday nights. We came up with a contract and agreed that we would bring our crowd back to Uncle Drew's club. Our plan worked and the people followed us! The following weekend we had Uncle Drew's club packed! After several parties at Uncle Drew's club, our first club owner, Mr. B, with whom we previously did business, wanted us back. Since we had relocated our venue, Mr. B's night club went back to its empty state. He realized the value of having us promote his parties, so we moved back to his place which was a better fit for the type of ambiance we wanted to party in. Uncle Drew was a bit upset, but he understood it was all business. We left Uncle Drew with a party formula that continued to reap his club success.

Now that our original club was rocking again, the success at Mr. B's club took place for several months. Unfortunately, just like before, Mr. B didn't want to renew his contract. He decided he wanted to go week to week with us, and we saw what he was trying to do. He wanted to confuse the city. He wanted to have some weekends where he made all of the profit and some weekends where we would share the profit; of course, we weren't going to have that! Realizing the greed and drama that was beginning to take place, we decided to part ways for good. In that type of situation, things can only get ugly and then everybody loses.

Surprisingly, there was another club that was opening up! What perfect timing this was? We are so lucky, I thought! I put my suit on and approached the new club owners. After a number of meetings and negotiating, we won their business. I was the one who did most of the negotiating with all of our deals and contracts. Our entertainment company was back in business, and this time we actually had two clubs in one. So we threw two different parties each night; one party for the grown and sexy, and one for those who were used to the urban scene. I'm talking about red suede and leather couches, chandeliers hanging all over the place, plasma TVs on the walls showing music videos, and a VIP area on a stage propped up for all to see. You see how Satan does; he needed to keep us in business so I could keep leading people astray!

This was a huge money-making opportunity here because the urban side of the club was also a sports bar and grill during the day. I assisted with the management aspects of the restaurant which only secured our relationship with these new owners. During the last year and a half, I left my corporate gig. I felt like I didn't need them anymore. My thinking was that I didn't want to wake up every morning and go to work for someone else when I could make a thousand bucks in one night partying with my friends.

### "The Love of my Life"

I'll never forget the first time I laid eyes on her. She worked for the same company that I did but at a different location. She walked into my rental car branch requesting to borrow some cars for her location. I thought to myself that her manager knew what he was doing by sending her, because I couldn't deny her anything. She could have walked in my office and said, *"Jeremy I need your whole fleet of cars,"* and I would have said, "Okay". Once she walked in my branch, I began to gather information on her from her coworkers; and in no time I knew all I needed to know.

Her name was Traci, and she had my full attention. After a brief conversation and discussion about the vehicles her office needed and when they would be returned, she left. Traci left my presence but not my mind. I thought about her every day after that. A few months later she walked in my office, and I found out that she had been transferred to my location. What a pleasant and unexpected surprise.

What was even more of a surprise to me was the way she carried herself. Traci was different from most of the women that I dated, and I quickly learned that something was special about her. Like most of the women I was involved with, Traci had goals, ambition, and she knew what she wanted to do in life. The difference that I felt was probably because my normal game didn't work on her; she was immune to everything I tried. After reality set in and I realized that I had no chances of getting with her, I respected the fact that we would just have a regular co-worker relationship. I soon found out that along with our love for food, we had a lot of things in common; and we became really good friends. Although I wanted to be more than just friends, like a wise man I took what I could get.

After I left my job, Traci and I still kept in contact. One day, out of the blue, she texted me and asked how I was doing. I told her all was well and that the business at the club was booming. She suggested that we should get together and hang out. I figured that she was talking about the whole office hanging out together because we always did things in a group; so I invited her and her girls out to the club that weekend. I told her that she and her friends would have their own booth, and drinks were on me. To my surprise after my response suggesting a group activity, she replied, *"I meant just you and me."* I thought to myself, *"Wait a minute, you mean you want to spend some time with just me?"* I couldn't believe it; she was actually going

She was like a breath of fresh air, and I was tired of the chase for different women.

to give me a shot. This was a shot I couldn't miss.

And there it sparked! Many good things came from that simple text message. She was like a breath of fresh air, and I was tired of the chase for different women. After my involvement with these women I felt just as empty inside emotionally as I'm sure they did. I was at a point in my life where I wanted more out of a woman beside sex. Might I add that sex was not an option with Traci which made my feelings for her grow even more.

Traci was so conservative that she wouldn't even sit on the same couch as I did when she would come over to my house to visit. She was so classy, yet down to earth and fun at the same time. We had a great connection. This woman had it all! She was smart; she could cook; and she kept the house clean. The more time we spent together, it became evident that she really cared about me as I did for her. We spent so much time together that we eventually began to date. Being with her was a rest haven from my crazy and corrupt lifestyle. After about a year of dating, we decided it would be best if she moved in with me. She spent so much time at my house she was rarely at her apartment; we eventually moved in together. She didn't really like the whole club scene; while I would be out handling business at the club, she would be home. I liked this persona about her because she was different from what I was used to at the club. I longed to come home to her where I felt true love and a sense of sanity.

I felt myself spiritually going deeper and deeper into a hole of darkness and despair. At the time I thought that Traci would be a way out. I looked to Traci for a spiritual refuge when I should have been looking to God. How often do we do that?

We think that a spouse or partner is what's missing in our life, when it's actually God. Nothing can fill that God void in our life but Christ Himself.

### "My involvement with Drugs"

I'll never forget how my involvement with drugs expanded. Through one of my best friends, I was connected to a good friend of his; I'd known this guy for some years, and one day while he was in town he stopped by my house. After a quick greeting, he tossed me a pound of weed and asked me if I could do something with it. I looked at the package, smiled, and assured him I could. He told me how much he wanted for it, and whatever else I make was profit for me.

The price for the weed was so good that I made two phone calls and sold a pound within the hour. Not only did I sell it quickly, but I made $400 profit for myself! Needless to say, he was pleased with my quick response and gave me two more pounds that night. By the next morning those were gone too. My *"connect"* was happy, and my pockets were too. You see those two years of management at my old job, I'd supplied many dealers with vehicles; now since they knew me and we had built relationships over the years, they trusted me to supply them with product.

Once my friend left town the following day, he connected me with the person who kept the work *"drugs."* He told me that he liked me and that he knew he could trust me. I could stop by whenever I wanted to get as much as I needed as long as I got the product off in a couple of days. To me this was a dream come true, because he would have anywhere from 20-40 pounds at a time. When I was young I said No to drugs, now

I have
no doubt
that it
was the
prayers
of my
mother
and
father
that kept
me.

I'm supplying the drug dealers.

I am disclosing this info to you to show you how the devil will set you up. When I was in high school I said I would never drink. Well, after playing with the devil, I not only drank but I became a drunk. I called myself a Christian when I was young and that I would never go to night clubs; not only did I attend the clubs and parties, but I promoted them. I told myself I wouldn't have sex till I was married, and now I was with a different woman every week. Lastly, I said I would never do drugs. Ha, not only did I do them, but I was addicted to them and sold them in large amounts. I lived a life that I am very ashamed of. It is only by the grace of God that I'm not dead, in prison, or have HIV/Aids! I have no doubt that it was the prayers of my mother and father that kept me.

At the moment life was good! I was making money at the club, and I was moving a large amount of work "drugs" around the city. Being big party promoters in the city, we knew the police well. In addition to security, we would pay the police under the table to watch our backs and hang out in the parking lot of the club to keep things in order. Everyone had their hands out wanting to make money. That was the name of the game, Money! Money! Money!

I was so consumed with the aspect of making money that I would bring the work *"drugs"* to the restaurant during the day so that if I got a call I didn't have to leave the club. I would have my buyers come to the restaurant and sit down like they were waiting on a to-go order. While they sat in the restaurant like a paying customer, I would cleverly put their product in a to-go box. I would then fix them a drink to go and send them on their way. My customers would walk right past a group of cops in the restaurant watching the game, and enjoying wings and fries. A whole pound of weed would slip right past them in a to-go box. At the time I thought this was both genius and hilarious, when it was actually flamboyant and cocky. It was only by the grace of God that I'm not writing this book from prison!

I operated like this for some time and never thought about the future. As long as my *"connect"* had the product, I would move it. The lifestyle that I was living was the kind you see in the movies. I lived the life of a rock star, only living for the next deal, party, or blunt. This lifestyle caused me personally to transform into something I wasn't really proud of. At the time I thought I was proud of my accomplishments but I was really empty inside. I knew the type of Christian background I came from, but felt I was in too deep to get out.

I tried to tell myself every day that I was handling business, and that I was only providing quality entertainment for the adults in the city. I would totally block out of my conscious what I was doing with the drugs. I ignored and blocked the Holy Spirit countless times, only for it to consistently press on my heart.

Every night before I would leave the house, and I would say this prayer to myself, *"Lord Save my Soul,"* then I would transform into what I needed to be that night. After a while the business at our new location began to struggle. The new club owners went bankrupt; and we had to loan them money to buy the alcohol for the parties. This, in return, gave us an opportunity to capitalize on the sales from the bar. Unfortunately, the situation from the club soon got worse. These club owners were the slowest, goofiest guys we had ever met; and when we realized the place was going under, we jumped ship.

# CHAPTER FIVE

## LAST CALL FOR ALCOHOL

### *"The end of the clubs and my drug connect"*

After the experience at the latest club ceased, we took a break for a while and took some vacation time in Atlanta. While in the Atlanta we hooked up with some of our friends there and partied for a bit. While in Atlanta the option came up for us to move the entertainment company there to expand our horizons. This made perfect sense to us at the time. We decided to take the same formula, but set it in effect in a larger city. As opposed to throwing parties in Huntsville with the maximum occupation at 400 people, we took this to Atlanta where the venues and clubs could hold anywhere from 600-2,000 people. We saw dollar signs and this opportunity seemed perfect. We felt that we'd outgrown Huntsville, so we figured we would take the entertainment company to a bigger city that could really appreciate the type of party we provided.

While in Atlanta networking, we hooked up with some millionaire Arabians who owned several clubs in the city. These guys knew all the top rappers like Young Jezzy, Solider Boy, Rick Ross, Ludacris, Shawty-Lo, and more. They were connected heavy in the rap industry, and we were their newest promoters.

When it came to money, my mentality was "I gotta get it; I gotta have it!"

Doors in Atlanta opened up for us just like every other club.

The devil has a way of opening doors for you; and God will allow you to walk through them. This is called the power of choice. We made a combined effort and put up some big money and began to go all in. I know that I personally had big plans to take on the city of Atlanta. I had plans of renting a condo there while renting my house in Huntsville. I was also thinking of how much work I could move from my connections in Atlanta. I looked at this situation, and my mouth began to water. I was ready for a big bite. When it came to money, my mentality was "I gotta get it; I gotta have it!" "For the love of money is the root of all kinds of evil. And some people, craving money, have wandered from the true faith and pierced themselves with many sorrows." 1 Timothy 6:10, NLT.

Surprisingly, things didn't work out quite how I thought. Actually, they didn't work out anything like how I thought. Things didn't make any sense; I mean we were throwing parties with Solider Boy, Shawty-Lo, and other rappers; and it just wasn't happening. I got to a point where I was mentally and financially tapped. I refused to put any more money in the entertainment company. I lost it all. I put all I had in this club business. I even used drug money to help fund these parties. This was a golden rule I was breaking, but I just knew the parties would be successful.

After my failures in Atlanta, I transitioned back to Huntsville; now all I wanted to do was move this work. It was hard because I had to get this product out without Traci finding out. I dug quite a big hole for myself with my drug connect. I was using the work and was selling it, but for a while I would take the money and invest it in the parties. Once the parties

How did
I get to
this point,
I was just
on top?
Now I'm
on the
bottom?

back fired on me, my "connect" called my phone asking for the money. Money I didn't have. I eventually spoke to him and explained the situation. I moved so much work for him in the past that he agreed to work with me on the payments. We were both waiting for this next shipment to come in. We expected this shipment to be the big one, especially me. The people I was getting my work from are not the type of people you screw over and just say I'm sorry. How did I get to this point, I was just on top? Now I'm on the bottom?

Mentally and emotionally I was going through a mid-life crisis. I felt like a failure. I had to come home and tell Traci that the parties flopped. I couldn't tell her about the drugs because I knew she would kill me herself. Some days I didn't even want to get out of the bed. I called my "connect" three times a day asking if the shipment had come in. He finally said, "I'll call you once it's in, just be ready! I later found out that the shipment got ambushed by the Feds, and there wasn't any product coming in. The transporter got caught and like everyone else, I was screwed.

Not only did I have this large debt to pay to my suppliers, but I also didn't have a dime to my name and no way to make money. My career corporate gig was gone; I didn't have any more parties to throw; my drug connect was gone for good; and no car to get around to look for another job. To make it all worse, I was running out of my own smoke stash. I used weed to control my depression and smoke my problems away. This was the first thing I needed in the morning, and the ONLY way I could sleep at night.

I felt like I was having an out-of-body experience; I couldn't believe how the last month turned out. I lost just about everything. Nothing was going right in my life. The only good thing I had to keep me going was Traci. All my other friends had ways to make money, but for me everything failed. These were some truly dark days that I was living in. The champagne stopped flowing; the music stopped playing; the party for me was over. Around this time I was probably feeling how the Prodigal son felt when he lost all of his money, and all his so-called friends were gone, and he had nowhere to turn to so we went and worked and ate with the pigs.

I remember waking up one morning not wanting to get out of bed. I hit complete rock bottom and was on the brink of tears. I didn't even want to live. I lay there on Sunday morning in bed; I could smell the breakfast Traci was cooking for me down stairs. As soon as I would step foot downstairs this is what I would hear "Good morning honey! Breakfast is almost ready. How did you do last night?" I couldn't find it within myself to tell her I failed. I couldn't tell her I lost it all. I couldn't tell her that I was a failure. I decided I wasn't getting out of bed that morning.

My cell phone soon rang, and I wasn't up for talking to anybody. Out of curiosity I wondered who was calling me so early in the morning, and to my surprise it was my Grandma Katie. This was a call I didn't really want to take because she was probably in an extra chipper mood, and I wasn't up for her usual motivational speech. My only plan of action was to ignore the call. The phone rang and rang, and I just looked and looked at it. After some time of contemplating, I thought that maybe I should call her back. She's normally right on time with things; and I could use some cheering up, I thought. Besides, Traci wasn't going to allow me to stay in bed all day anyway, so

I called her back.

The conversation started off regular but my depression was all in my voice. I tried my best to sound regular, but she could see right through me. She asked why was my voice cracking and inquired what was wrong. I told her it was nothing; but she insisted that Grammy knows when something is wrong. I just told her that I was going through a really rough time and that I needed prayer. Isn't it something how we only want to pray to God when things are going wrong. After our disobedience, God will allow things to go wrong so that we come back to Him; and every time He's standing there with open arms.

My grandmother soon began to motivate and minister to me. Our conversation soon brought me to tears. After she prayed with me, I thanked her and I mentioned how this call was right on time. I asked her how she knew to call me. She said, "Grandson, I didn't call you! I was driving down the road, and I was calling my friend and dialed your number by accident. I immediately hung up and dialed the right number." I said, "But Grandma that makes no sense because on my end the phone rang a bunch of times. I know because I sat there and watched the call go to voice-mail. My grandmother then began to cry and said, "Grandson, that wasn't me calling you; that was the Holy Spirit, and He's been calling you for a long time now."

This broke me all the way down. I couldn't believe it. This made absolutely no sense to me. I didn't understand at the moment what was taking place. After that experience, I tried my best to change my lifestyle. I started to go to church, and I even stopped listening to rap music. There was this video documentary that came out called the "Jay-Z Deception" that discussed the satanic worship behind rap music and the secular music industry as a whole. This was something that was clear to see, and I began to have distaste for this type of music.

I was still living in sin, smoking, and waiting for my *"connect"* to call me, but I was done with rap music. You see, I wasn't trying to give God my all. All too often we try to compromise with God. We tell Him the things we are going to get rid of and the things we plan to keep. Those next few weeks just got darker and darker, and I couldn't see the light at the end of the tunnel. My days were filled with applying for jobs online, lifting weights, and smoking my weed. This didn't seem like a promising future, but that's all I had.

# CHAPTER SIX

## THE RIDE OF MY LIFE

### *"Road Trip"*

Lost doesn't describe what I was. I lost my identity, my money, my career, my self esteem, my pride, my dignity, and so much more. I lost all of these things for self pleasure, gratification, greed, lust, money, popularity; but I wasn't willing to lose my soul.  God has a way of doing things that man will never understand. That's why we call Him God.  *"For my thoughts are not your thoughts, neither are your ways my ways, saith the LORD. For as the heavens are higher than the earth, so are my ways higher than your ways, and my thoughts than your thoughts."* Isaiah 55:8, 9, KJV.

One day while I was at home watching TV, I got a call from my grandfather. Now this was from my dad's father who is also a minister.  I knew he was in town, so I answered to see what he needed.  During our phone conversation, he basically asked if I still had some colleagues from my old job, because he needed a way to get back home. He then told me how his car was acting up, and that he, my grandmother Rose, and my aunt Kim were going to do a one-way rental to South Carolina. Realizing how expensive the one-way rental would be and considering I had nothing else to do, I instantly offered to take them to South Carolina. I would drive back and return the rental car myself. Happy to receive the offer, my grandfather accepted and the date was set.

After I got off the phone with my grandfather, Traci asked if I were really going to take them to South Carolina and then drive the car back. I told her I might; and she laughed and said, *"It's too late now; you've already committed to it."* Wow! Now I'm second guessing my offer. I just volunteered to do something I really didn't want to do, and before really analyzing and thinking about it, I blurted out the offer to take this road trip. Since the commitment was made, I tried to look on the bright side. My parents lived about a hour from where my grandparents lived, so the plan was to stop there that evening and spend the night with them and hang out for a bit.

The day came when it was time for the road trip. This was a trip I really didn't want to take nor was I mentally prepared for it. The worse part of the situation was I couldn't take my medicine "weed" during the trip. You see, one thing I loved to do during solo road trips was driving down the open road smoking some good green. This, of course, couldn't take place because I was driving my family out of state. While renting the car, I repeatedly told myself that I could do this and that it would only be a day or so without my meds.

The time was here! My grandfather tossed me the keys and said, *"Let's do it!"* We loaded the car, said a prayer, and were headed to South Carolina. The first hour of the trip was rough. I kept dwelling on the fact that I was confined to do seven hours of hard labor behind the driver's seat without a cigarette or beer. After a while I calmed down, and we all began to talk.

The four of us spoke about all sorts of things during the beginning of the trip. After a while the girls (my grandma Rose and Kim) were asleep in the back seat and it was just me and my grandfather in the front talking. Somehow we got on the topic of the church and the last days. We discussed how the world was coming to an end and how the youth of today are just lost. I'm thinking to myself *"Yeah, we are lost."* I soon asked my grandfather a question, and when it came out of my mouth I regretted it. I asked *"Who is going to reach the youth of today, who's going to take this last day message to them?"* His response to me was *"You are!"* I swallowed deeply, and there was a weird awkward silence in the car. After this brief awkward moment, the conversation went on and we soon made it to our destination.

After dropping them off and unloading the car, I made my way back on the road to knock out another hour or so to make it to my parents' home. Upon arrival they greeted me warmly, and we ate and talked. I got to see my late grandmother Patricia McCormick, my sister Ashley, and her two boys, and my mom and dad. We had a good time. I even decided to take back to Huntsville my sister's oldest son, Nickolas, to stay for a week or so with Traci and me. Later that night as we were winding down, I was in my parent's room lying across the end of their bed, when we entered into an interesting conversation. It was about politics, the illuminati, and the last days, and so forth. The basis of the conversation was how we all need to be ready when the Lord comes again. After that thought-provoking conversation, I called it a night. The only way that I could fight the urges and strong desire for tobacco and weed was to just try and sleep it off; after all, I was exhausted from the trip so rest was what I needed.

### "God's Secret Covert Mission to save my SOUL"

The next morning I grabbed my nephew, loaded the car, said my good-byes to the family and I was off! The night before my mother told me to stop in Atlanta for a bit and take my Grandma Katie out for lunch. Even though this was conflicting with my plans of indulging in my habits, I agreed. The plan was to stop in Atlanta, and after lunch with my Grammy I could have a quick smoke then finish the trip home. Things didn't quite turn out like I planned. You see that was my plan, but not God's plan.

How often do we think we have life all figured out. All too often we have plans of our own, only to find out that this is not what God has in store for us. I was about one hour from Atlanta when I called my grandmother to schedule our soon-appointed lunch date. To my surprise, she informed me that she was on the way to a doctor's appointment and that she had an hour drive to get there. I said, *"It's OK, I understand."* I figured I'd see her next time. Her response to me while laughing was, *"You're driving, and I'm driving; what's up? Let's talk."*

I laughed at the classic enthusiasm she has for life and we began to talk. The conversation was great as usual. It's always great to talk to my grandmother because she has been the spiritual pillar in our family since Mama Lola, my great grandmother, passed. One thing I can say about my grandma Katie…She can talk. I know because she's just like me, and I can talk. Grammy doesn't just talk; she has always been a voice for the Holy Spirit. We rarely have regular conversations. Most of our conversations are spirit filled, even when I didn't want them to be. During this conversation, we talked about her experience in Atlanta and mine in Huntsville. I don't think I nor my grandmother knew what was about to take place on this call.

The discussion between my grandma Katie and I took an interesting turn. She began to tell me exactly where I was in life. She began to tell me that I was truly unhappy and that God didn't want that for me. She began to tell me that I wasn't just a regular person, and that she expected great things from me.

My Grandmother reminded me of my experience preaching at Madison Mission SDA Church. She asked: *"What happened to that Jeremy. I know you still have it in you."* She said that my rebellion was why things were not going right for me! She told me that I was chosen and that God's going to do great things with me, and that she could see me preaching before Madison Mission again in the future. She said that I should stop running; that I would never have true peace until I gave it all to God. The whole time she was saying these things, I was thinking hard about what she was saying. Honestly, everything she said made sense in a way.

The tone that she was talking with me was one of sternness and love. Our conversation had kind of a tough love type of feel. The whole time she is talking to me I had a voice in my head saying, *"She just doesn't understand,"* and *"You can just quit everything and turn your life around."* These thoughts plagued my mind during the majority of our conversation. There was one thing that my grandma Katie disclosed to me that really hit home. She talked about Blessing Blockers, and how everyone at some point in their life has Blessing Blockers.

My grandmother said that Blessing Blockers where things

in our life that we must get rid of before God can have his way with us. Until we get rid of these Blessing Blockers, we will remain in the same position. My position was one of darkness. Even when things were going right I was still living in darkness while feeling an artificial joy.

By now the Holy Spirit is channeling from her lips through her phone, bouncing off the phone towers, dropping down through my cell into my ears and straight to my heart. I was so overwhelmed, heart heavy with burden, I couldn't hold back. My eyes began to get watery, and this wet stuff started to flow down from my eyes continuously. My heart was so open to the Spirit I forgot I was even driving. The car just seemed to float down the highway while the Spirit worked on my heart. We both began to cry as my grandmother told me that she hadn't given up on me. That meant so much because right before she said that, my thoughts were *"But I've done too much; God doesn't want me."* She said the opposite. She told me that God had spared me for a reason and to stop fighting Him.

This conversation was something that neither one of us expected. She told me to go home and go to my prayer closet and have a one-on-one conversation with God and to give Him my all. My all means the good, the bad, and the ugly. After praying with me we both expressed how much we loved each other and soon parted from the phone. It boggled my mind how this conversation came to be. I soon realized that what just took place was a Special Operation/Secret Covert Mission put in place to save my soul. This was a well executed plan by the Holy Spirit. If you don't see how, let me refresh your memory and break this down to you.

One main reason why prodigals, the lost, strays, whatever

While we are in our mess, the Holy Spirit never left us; we just aren't receptive to His voice.

you want to call us, don't listen and truly receive the Holy Spirit is because our Spiritual receptors are blocked. Mankind, the human race was made in God's image. We were made to commune with God. While we are in our mess, the Holy Spirit doesn't leave us; we 're just not receptive to His voice.

"*So God created man in his own image, in the image of God created he him; male and female created he them.*" Genesis 1:27, KJV. Now listen to what Paul says in Hebrews 2:7, "*Thou madest him a little lower than the angels; thou crownedst him with glory and honor, and didst set him over the works of thy hands.*" KJV. With pure minds and heart, we are connected to God in a special way. What tends to make the communication foggy, unclear or distorted, is when we put intoxicants in our body. Intoxicants can be anything from narcotics, tobacco, alcohol, negative music, etc.

You see, we all have spiritual receptors in our brain which allow us to stay connected to our higher power which is through the Holy Spirit. When we have these pollutants in our body, we are not nearly connected with the Holy Spirit how we should. Notice that I said "*nearly*" when you hear that little voice telling you not to do something wrong, or something tugs at your heart when it's appeal time in church, that's the Holy Spirit!

The special mission that God put in motion for me was executed perfectly. First, he put me in a position away from my normal settings. I didn't have this conversation with my grandmother while I was at home on my couch. He made it so that I didn't have any of my normal pollutants like my cigarettes, weed, alcohol, etc., in my body. So this means that I was going on a record of about 36 hours straight with nothing in my system.

FROM PRODIGAL TO PRODIGY

Another thing that wasn't clouding my mind was rap music or any other form of music that can be harmful to my spirit. Now I'm not attacking rap music, and I don't believe that all rap music is bad. When it comes to secular music, it depends on the message of the music. My concerns were not so much how the music was delivered, but the message that was being delivered. For some it may be rock or heavy metal, but for me I loved rap music. Since there was a new-found distaste for most rap music and certain artists, I wasn't listening to any.

So here I am driving down the road taking the ride of my life That's why I call this chapter "The ride of my Life" because when I got to my destination, I decided what my final destination would be, which was Heaven! I can see it now. This was a collaboration between God, the Father, God, the Son, God, the Holy Spirit, and my guardian angel. I can just see it now; my angels are flying next to my car, and going through the check list with God.

The Father... "No marijuana, right?"
My Guardian Angel... "Check."
The Father... "System all clear of tobacco?"
My Guardian Angel... "Check."
The Father... "Alcohol?"
Guardian Angel... "All Clear."
The Father... "What about music?"
My Guardian Angel... "Gospel music is playing, Sir."
The Father... "OK, so he should be receptive to the Holy Spirit?"
My Guardian Angel... "That's a 10-4."
The Father... "OK, make sure his grandmother is free for

*the call."*

My Guardian Angel… *"You set her appointment with the doctor's office weeks ago"*

The Father… *"OK, they've been talking for about 10 minutes now; GO Holy Spirit, GO!!!"*

And you know the part that God, the Son, Jesus Christ, played? Jesus made all of this possible. That day on Calvary He paid it all. Over 2000 years ago Jesus died for my sins. *"For God so loved the world that he gave his one and only Son, that whoever believes in him shall not perish but have eternal life."* John 3:16, NIV.

What type of deep true love that is that a man would lay down his life for a friend? Let's look at the plan of redemption a little closer. Jesus came to pay the price for our sins. Jesus lived a life free from sin. Jesus was innocent yet He gave His life so that the plan of Salvation would be in place. Romans 6:23 says that *"the Wages of sin is death, but the gift of God is Eternal life through Jesus Christ our Lord."* With what is stated here in Romans, we should all be doomed for hell's fire, unless we except Christ as our Savior. We have all fallen short of the glory of God, and have sinned throughout our lives.

We were born into a sinful world with centuries of sinful characteristics embedded in our character traits. The great news is that Eternal life is free for all who claim Jesus. His Blood that was shed on Calvary is payment enough to wash our sins white as snow! No man could take Christ life but by Him laying down His life, He's saying, *"I accept your apology, and salvation for you is free. I've already paid the price for your sins on Calvary!"* Thank You, Jesus!!!!

# CHAPTER SEVEN

**LIFE AFTER DEATH**

*"To die of the flesh is to live in the Spirit"*

After getting off the phone with my grandma Katie I had about a three-hour drive until I made it back home. My heart was heavy during the remainder of the drive home. I thought and thought and thought about me really taking this life-changing step in the right direction. I was nervous and scared of this well-needed change of lifestyle. I was literally scared to go all the way with Christ. Let me share with you some of my thoughts that were going on in my head at the time.

1. What are people going to think?
2. What if I back track and slip up and sin?
3. What if I can't do it?
4. I can't just stop smoking?
5. My *"connect"* is going to call me any day, and I need this money!

Now these were my thoughts after the tears dried, and I'm in the car silently driving. I looked in the rear view mirror and was doing some soul searching. There were these voices that were telling me to wait. I knew what I needed to do, but I felt unworthy. These thoughts that were going through my head were negative and from the devil himself telling me I couldn't change my ways. I felt like I'd gone so far down in the wrong direction, there was no turning around for me. These were the responses from God to each question or doubtful thoughts that the enemy gave.

1. Who cares what people think? This is your life and soul salvation!
2. You will fall down, but you'll get up! Prov. 24:16
3. You can't do it alone. BUT with my help, you can!
4. Phil. 4:13: *"I can do ALL things through Christ who strengthens me."*
5. Psalm 27:1: *"The LORD is my light and my salvation; whom shall I fear? The LORD is the strength of my life; of whom shall I be afraid?"*

You see the enemy was around during this conversation; and he didn't like how the Holy Spirit was working. Once the conversation ended, Satan instantly began to do what he does best, which is bring discouragement and deception to your mind. You see he knows the power we have when we call on the name Jesus. He gave me multiple excuses and reasons not to give my life completely to God. Every time I would get a doubtful thought, the Holy Spirit would remind me that God is my strong tower and that he would never give me more than I could bear.

The comfort, support, encouragement and prayers that I received from my mother were recalled to my memory. The principles and training my father instilled in me as a young boy came back to mind during that three-hour drive home. I thought about all the times I came close to death and how God spared my life over and over again. I knew deep down inside that if I continued down that path of rejecting Christ and the

I was so filled with
the Spirit that at that
moment I was Set
Free!

FROM PRODIGAL TO PRODIGY

life He has for me I would soon lose my soul. God continued to work on my heart, and during the drive home I came to the conclusion that me and my house would serve the Lord.

This wasn't an easy decision at all. You see during the ride to Huntsville from Atlanta, I still had some green with me. Those last three hours I held that sack of weed in my hand contemplating what to do with it. Every so often, I would take a sniff of the sack. You see, it had almost been two days, and I was long overdue for my medicine and the Spirit was telling me to throw it out the window. The mere thought of me throwing the green out seemed so absurd to me that I just couldn't. My thoughts were: *"What if I get home and regret it?"* I thought that I won't be able sleep that night and would be miserable, angry, and cranky. I put my meds back in my pocket and wiped my nervous and sweaty hands on the side of my pants.

I soon made it home and was greeted by my lovely girlfriend Traci with a kiss and dinner. I soon got my nephew Nickolas settled and began to tell Traci about what had just taken place during my ride from Atlanta. Traci told me that she was happy for me and that she would support me; but I could tell from the look in her eyes that she wanted to believe me, but there was some doubt. I can't blame her for having some doubt considering the type of lifestyle I was living. We talked more; then she made her way upstairs to get Nick settled in bed.

While Traci is upstairs I'm downstairs sitting with a gorilla in the room. What's the gorilla you ask? The gorilla in the room was the sack of green in my pocket. What do I do with it? I've been waiting to blow this since I left two days ago. So here's the devil again trying to bargain with me. I listened and came to the conclusion that if I was going to stop smoking then I would go out with a bang. My plan was to smoke all of it at once, so I went through my normal preparations, and I was off to my normal smoke section of the house which was my garage. On the way to the garage I stopped in the kitchen to pour me a glass of wine to complement my voyage.

What took place next was a first time for me ever. I took my seat, put my feet up and light a cigarette to prepare my body to receive my medicine. After a few puffs, it wasn't sitting right in my system, and I figured it had just been two days too long. After a few hits, the weed seemed weird, and made me feel uncomfortable; so I took a sip of my merlot to settle my nerves and proceeded on my voyage; but something was different, the weed wasn't sitting right with me or my soul!

My body was rejecting all of the pollutants I was putting in it. I was so filled with the Spirit that at that moment I was Set Free! I am telling you the 100% truth. This is just how it happened. God took the urge from me at that moment. I was so filled with the Holy Spirit, I felt free from my bondage. Alcohol that had such a strong hold on me for so many years no longer had me bound. Weed that I needed in the morning, during the day, and at night to sleep was now irrelevant. The cigarettes I so frequently resorted to, no longer calmed my nerves, but now gave me a headache! I knew then that God was truly in the miracle-working business.

You see, Satan wanted me to have my so called *"last blunt,"* and God allowed me to try it again to show me I was changed! I thought about me smoking weed for so long, that I figured my body wanted it and needed it to function. The truth is that during my drive home when I accepted God and made my mind up to follow Him, I had the victory over sin. At that

Satan will try
his hardest to
discourage and
destroy you!

FROM PRODIGAL TO PRODIGY

moment I took that blunt that was on the forefront of my mind and threw it in my glass of wine. I left the garage and rejoiced at this miraculous miracle. I prayed to God and gave Him thanks, and went upstairs to bed and slept like a baby!

The next morning was a rough one for me. Not from the desire for my usual habits, but from the fear of failure. I really wanted to give God my all; and I was scared of falling into sin again. My heart that morning was heavier than it ever was. I was pleased to get a call from my brother Daryl who was asking me to bring my nephew to campus so they could spend the day together. I was relieved at the request because I needed some time alone to think and pray.

I had such a fear of failure that I really wanted to crawl under a rock. It felt so good to be free, and I didn't want to lose this feeling. The feeling I had last night conquering those addictions felt so good, I feared the possibilities of slipping and losing God. I got myself and Nick together, and we headed to campus. The ride to Oakwood seemed like it was taking forever. The enemy was on my head and heart heavy. The same questions and doubt kept coming to mind, and it was almost more than I could bear.

Satan will try his hardest to discourage and destroy you! When this happens you feel overwhelmed and sometimes alone. All you can do in this instance is cry out to God. We must believe in the power of prayer. Honestly, I wasn't feeling God's power or strength at that time. I felt abandoned, scared, lonely, and was on the verge of giving up. The enemy kept telling me, *"Look, no one does a 180 instantly; I know you want to change; just do it gradually."* These were the depressing thoughts going on in my head.

God wants so much more for our lives; yet being blind to His love, we settle for temporary fulfillment.

I soon arrived at Oakwood College Church and swiftly grabbed my nephew out of the car. My plan was to locate either David or Daryl to drop off Nick and then head back home to be alone. It was a Tuesday and my brothers were in chapel; so I went to the church to find them. Once I walked in the church I saw my brothers, and Nick ran to greet his uncles. While turning around to make a quick exit out of the overly crowded Church lobby, my eyes landed on someone. It was my good friend Java!

What a shock to see Java at this time in my life. I knew that he could relate to me wanting to change my life because he too did a complete sudden 180 while we were in school. Immediately, I ran to him, and while we embraced each other, I broke down crying. I told Java my plans on getting re-baptized. These tears that washed my face were tears of joy.

Running into Java like that was a clear sign from the Lord. Upon seeing Java, God showed me that you can make a drastic and sudden change; He had done it in Java's life! I stood there in the middle of that church with Java for a few minutes crying while testifying of the goodness of the Lord. I didn't care who was looking at me, I felt free!!! The way I felt on the way to the church was reversed by God. Java and I prayed together, and then parted ways. On the ride home I felt so good. I felt like I truly gave it all to the Lord.

It was confession time. I instantly called my father and began to disclose my life from the past 10 years. It was important that my dad knew where God brought me from, so I disclosed a decent amount of information from my wicked past. I thought I was confessing my sins to him, but my father's response to my so-called confession session was, *"Son, I knew what you were into. Your mother and I have been praying for your failure the whole time because we knew God would bring you back home."* This was so shocking to me because they never acted like they knew. I would have never known they knew the type of lifestyle I was living because they always treated me with love. Does this remind you of anybody? We can get off track, but God still loves us no matter how deep in sin we go or what we do. God wants so much more for our lives; yet being blind to His love, we settle for temporary fulfillment. To any parents reading this book, be encouraged! Regardless of what your children are doing, it's important that you continue to pray, encourage, and love them just as Christ does us. Far too often you may want to write your children off, but that's not the answer. Prayer is powerful; it changes things.

We all fall short of the glory of God; but He is always there for us. What if God wrote you off because of your sins? In God's eyes all sins are equal; and believe it or not, Christ wants your children saved just as much if not more than you do. James 5:16 says that *"Therefore confess your sins to each other and pray for each other so that you may be healed. The prayer of a righteous man is powerful and effective."* James 5: 16 NIV.

My father and I continued to talk for some time while making plans for my baptism. By now I have made it back home, and I'm sitting on my front porch talking to my dad. Out of nowhere my neighbor comes over to me and hands me some weed, tells me to enjoy it, and proceeded to walk back to his house. Not only was the green for free, but it was wrapped up and ready to burn!

Delayed with shock, I called after him and handed it back to him and said, *"Thanks, but no thanks."* He gave me a blank stare and asked if I was sure. I told him that I didn't smoke anymore and with a puzzled look, he apologized and said, *"Congrats!"* I then told my dad what just took place. He could hear it in my voice I was excited that I passed my first temptation test. My father warned me that there would be plenty more where that came from. We set the date for my baptism, prayed together, and ended our call.

Two weeks later Traci and I traveled to Florence, South Carolina, to fulfill my appointment with the baptismal pool. I'll never forget that day! I was anxious and nervous. I met other brothers who had also taken their stand for baptism. As we prepared for the water, we shared our testimonies with one another. One guy had been addicted to crack cocaine for over ten years. The other guy hustled for years and had experiences with drugs as well. Both of these guys that I was getting were older than me. I praise God for grace and mercy. We along with the other baptismal candidates stood before the church and had our vows read to us and after accepting the charge, the church began to sing as we made our way to the pool.

This was a great day seeing Traci, my sister Ashley, and my Mom on the front row shedding tears of joy for me. I was the last person to go into the baptismal pool. While the person before me was going down in the water I had a few seconds alone with God, and I thanked Him for this day. You know how they say before you die your life flashes before your eyes? Well, that's what happened to me. Getting ready to die of self and life in Christ, I took a moment and reflected on my old life that God delivered me from. I knew then that after this next moment, I'd never be the same again.

My turn soon came, and when I stepped into the pool, the

It's amazing
what obedience
will do to your
life and spirit.

FROM PRODIGAL TO PRODIGY

church began to shout! The church knew the Prodigal son had returned home.  As my father began to express his love for me and gratification to God, all I could do was bury my head in his chest and cry. A few moments later, I was baptized in the name of the Father, Son, and Holy Spirit!  Coming up out of the water a new man, my father and I both hugged and wept together.  October 17, 2009, was a good day because it was the day I began to die of my fleshy ways and live in the Spirit of God.  My girlfriend Traci soon joined the church and got rebaptized as well.  I could see the Holy Spirit doing something great within both us.  It's amazing what obedience will do to your life and spirit.

I had no idea
I was about to
embark on a
spiritual journey
that would take
me higher and
higher.

# CHAPTER EIGHT

## REBUILDING

### *"Wedding Bells"*

The next day after my baptism Traci and I drove back to Huntsville, AL. When we arrived home, I remember asking myself, *"What Now?"* I had no idea what was about to take place within my life. I thought that since I was baptized I was right where God wanted me to be. I had no idea I was about to embark on a spiritual journey that would take me higher and higher. About a week or so from the baptism, my father called me one night to check on me. We spoke for a while; then he began to ask me how my spiritual walk was going. I implied that I was strong and that the urges were still there, but told him that I was good. Even though the baptism was fresh, I still had the power from God over my habits of alcohol and marijuana.

From the conversation I was having with my dad I could tell something troubled him. He asked me if he could discuss something with me and my reply was, *"Of course!"* He asked if he could be frank with me, and I said, *"Please do."* He said that God wants your all. I told him I knew that. He said: *"That means you have to let go of all of your sins."* He went on to say how stopping the clubbing and dealing drugs, using and abusing the intoxicants is good, but pre-marital sex is a sin as well.

My response to this was *"Come on dad, no sex?....I can't just stop having sex."* He said, *"So basically you are saying that God can take away your other addictions, but He can't take away all of your addictions?"* He told me that I was basically saying that God is good, but He's not great and all powerful. My response to this was that I love Traci, and it's not like were sleeping around; we've built a life together. I can't just move out." His response was that I needed to marry her or move out. He reminded me how the enemy operates. He said that the devil will use that one sin I was holding on to and the next thing you know is you'll be right back to where you started. Now this scared me because I was tired of the spiritual roller coaster, I needed something real!

This was a conversation that I wasn't too crazy about. I was still in a bit of denial and doubt to the whole fact that I was living in sin. I felt like since I was only sleeping with the woman I loved it was OK. This is called fornication. *"Do you not know that the unrighteous will not inherit the kingdom of God? Do not be deceived. Neither fornicators, nor idolaters, nor adulterers, nor homosexuals, nor sodomites, nor thieves, nor covetous, nor drunkards, nor revilers, nor extortioners will inherit the kingdom of God."* 1 Corinthians 6:9, 10, NKJV.

My dad and I talked the whole night about the pros and cons of getting married. To be honest, I knew what move to make; I was just scared. Traci and I worked together before we began to date. We dated and lived together for approximately two years. This woman was with me when I was on top and at the bottom, through the good and the bad, through thick and thin, and I have no doubt that her prayers contributed to where

I am today.

Traci was always there and I realized I wanted her to always be there. I had no doubt she would be a great wife and an amazing mother to our children, I was just scared of doing the right thing. I think the real reason this pill was hard to swallow was because my money was short, and I couldn't do for her what I wanted to. My father then told me to pray about it, like he does with most things, *"which works"* and we got off the phone and called it a night.

The next day for some strange reason I actually told Traci what my father and I discussed the night before. We talked on the phone while she was at work and she asked me what conclusion I came to. I told her plainly that I wasn't ready to get married. That night when Traci came home I could tell something was wrong. We sat on the couch to discuss how our days went and the conversation that we had earlier came up again. As she tried to fight back her tears of disappointment, she told me how she felt about the situation. She said that she didn't understand what was wrong with her for me not to want to marry her. She told me how much she loved me, and how faithful and committed she was; she just didn't understand why I wouldn't want to marry her. She also questioned my love for her.

While laughing I tried to calm her down and assured her that she had things all wrong. I told her that I loved her so much, but I didn't want to rush anything because she deserved more. I assured her that when I was more financially stable, I would get her a big ring and do things right. Traci's response to that was that she didn't need a ring as long as she had me! I said, *"Really?"* She said, *"Yes!"* I laughed and said, *"Well let's do*

Sex was made for man and woman in the union they have with God.

FROM PRODIGAL TO PRODIGY

*it, let's get married!"* I dropped to one knee and right there on the spot asked her to marry me, and she accepted! We instantly got on the phone and told our close family and friends of the good news!

With out a doubt our families were happy with the news of us being engaged. The plan was for us to have a small inexpensive wedding and to have it soon. There was only one problem with this picture. I had to call Traci's Mom and ask for her hand in marriage. Her mother and I had a good relationship but you see, I was unemployed and I dreaded the question of finances! I called my father and told him of the soon-to-be- much needed conversation with Traci's mom. My dad found this really funny due to my unemployment situation; yet he agreed this was a conversation that needed to happen.

With my heart beating out of my chest, I called Traci's mother "Momma Deb" and proclaimed my love for her daughter. Her response was *"Jeremy, that's nice and all but how are you going to provide for her and you don't have a job."* I laughed and told her that my dad told me to expect that question. She laughed as well for a second, then got back serious and asked: *"Well, how are you going to provide for my daughter?"* I cleared my throat and assured her that since we were doing things the right way and putting God first in our lives, I had no doubt that He would bless our union and provide me with a job. I assured her that by the time the wedding came around I would be working. She faithfully granted me permission.

### *"My Battles with Flesh"*

You ever think you know something only to find out later that you had no idea of it? That's what I was going through.

You see Traci and I decided to get married for three reasons: Love, Commitment, and Loyalty. We knew that God had us in each other's lives for a reason. It was extremely important for us both to do things the right way; which was to refrain from sex before marriage which was four months away. I severely underestimated my desire and addiction to lust and sex. I was having a hard time even grasping the concept of not being able to lay with the woman I love. I figured that since she was the one I was going to marry, it was OK.

My experience with women came well before my experiences with some of the other addictions in my life. From the time I first became sexually active, I can't recall going more than a week without some type of sexual encounter. I began to be accustomed to sex and a deep love for women. Lust is something that all males battle with. There is nothing wrong with sex, but we must look at the context that sex was made in. Sex was made for man and woman in the union they have with God. Sex should be a holy and high experience that you share with the husband or wife that God gave you. *"Therefore shall a man leave his father and his mother, and shall cleave unto his wife: and they shall be one flesh."* Gen 2:24, KJV. When the bible says "Cleave unto his wife," it is speaking of the act of sex. Think about this for a moment. When you are in the act of sexual intercourse, the male and female are in the process of insertion, which is becoming one in body and spirit. Once you become married, you are detaching from your parents and in order for you to start your own family, you must attach, *"Cleave"* unto your spouse.

The issue that I was dealing with was bigger than the reason why. I understood that sex before marriage was what the Bible calls *"fornication."* I knew that fornication was wrong. The Bible makes it really plain in 1 Corinthians 6:9-10. My struggle was refraining from the action. I had to live with Traci and all her beauty, and refrain from sexual activities. This was new for me. I came to a close reality how much my lustful desires had a strong hold on me. These next four months would be a time to remember. Traci and I discussed this often, and we had no choice but to pray to God to give us the power to hold true to our commitment with Him. It was in the act of abstinence that I grew closer to God spiritually and Traci mentally.

Reflecting on what my father suggested to me about limiting God on what He can do, I had to claim that this was an accomplishment that I could achieve. Throughout life we must realize that we can accomplish anything. In order for us to be successful in situations, it's important that we put ourselves in successful positions. We must set ourselves up for success in everything we do. If you are living with your friend, and you are trying to win the battle over pre-marital sex, there are certain things you shouldn't do.

If I were you, I would stay away from strip clubs. Cut out music that would so called, *"put you in the mood"* as well as monitor what you watch on TV. I would also avoid being around while your spouse changes her clothes. You may also have to sleep in separate beds. You want to avoid these things so that you don't put yourself in compromising situations. If you can't, you can always go to the courthouse. *"But if they cannot control themselves, they should marry, for it is better to marry than to burn with passion."* 1 Corinthians 7:9, NIV. The Bible makes everything plain. This scripture here is plainly saying that if you can't control your hormones and practice abstinence till the wedding day, go to the court house and make it official.

This time of abstinence for me was more than me just learning to control my hormones. This was a cleansing of spirit and character. I had such a reckless sexual lifestyle, God had to take me through an interesting process to prepare me to be the man He wanted for Traci. My mind and soul were so polluted with women of the past that this time of abstinence was sexually reprogramming for me. Sexual intercourse, the act of "cleaving" with your spouse, is a Holy and sacred ceremony that has been perverted in every way. I remember calling my dad one day after the first month, complaining of some manly pains I was experiencing. After I shared with him the physical and mental pains I was experiencing, he disclosed to me what was taking place within my life and body.

My dad explained to me the process a potter goes through to turn a clay vase or bowl into something else. He said that since the vase has been hardened and seared through the fire, it needed to be broken down into real fine pieces; and that once the potter has put the vase through a fine grinding process, he then adds water to the mixture, and the results is clay. The clay is now able to be remolded and shaped into what the potter wants it to be! My father said that once the potter has shaped the clay, he puts it through the fire so that it can be seared "hardened". Although the seared process can be hot, this is what must be done so that it can be used effectively.

My father went on to relate the process a potter does to remold his clay to what our Heavenly Father does when He wants to remold us for His use. This is the same thing that takes place in our Christian walk. Sometimes the devil uses us for so long, we must go through this remolding process. In order for God to use us, He has to remold us. But before He could remold us, He has to break us all the way down!

After God breaks you down and grinds you up, He adds water to you *"baptism,"* then He reshapes you. After God grinds us down fine, adds water to our lives and remolds us, we must then go through the fire. Though the fire is hot, it's there to make us spiritually hard and strong so that like the pot or vase, we can be used. Is there a fire in your life? Have you decided to give God your all but it seems like your situation is getting hotter? God allows hard times to come so that you can find your strength in Him!

After realizing this I knew I wanted to be a vessel for God; so I embraced the fire. You see like a pot being turned into a vessel, God broke me down by allowing me to lose everything. God knew that with my stubbornness, He had to strip me of everything and humble me so that He could use me. In order for God to save us He has to Break us! Once God broke me down, He had to grind me up and add water to my life. After being baptized, He told me what He wanted in my life, and He remolded me to be the man He wanted me to be. Now God just needs to sear me so He puts me through some tests. As I overcome the fire, my Test soon turns into Testimonies!

My father told me to hang in there and to seek God during those times of discomfort and frustration. This was a time when I had to completely rely on God. I think that due to my promiscuous, prodigal lifestyle, I was damaged mentally, sexually, and spiritually. Before God could give me my wife, there were things within my spirit, personality, and character He had to get right.

### *"Waiting on the Lord"*

My lifestyle was so different from what it was before. This was truly a breaking, yet building point for me. Everything that I used to escape to for temporary comfort was now gone. I had to totally rely on the Lord. If I was in a bad mood, I wasn't turning to weed. If I needed to calm my nerves, I didn't turn to tobacco. If I had a long day and wanted to wind down, there was no alcohol. I was stripped of all of my deadly intoxicants that offered temporary relief. God wanted to show me that He could fill every void, every need, every desire, and every want in my life. Not only can God fill those voids in your life but those voids are truly fulfilled.

We were made to worship and commune with God. Since He is our Creator, His spirit is within all of us. When we have a void in our lives we are missing a true relationship with Him. That emptiness that we feel when the music stops, or your high comes down and no one is around, is God's space that He wants to fill. Many times we come to the conclusion that we need a significant other in our life to make us complete and whole when all we need is God. He wants to fill every void in your life, but you must let Him. And in order for Him to come in and fill those voids, you must make room in your heart. That means there are some things you must give up so that God can inhabit that space and make you whole again.

There was another thing I was working on, and the problem was that "I" was working on it when I should have given it to God. I needed a job! I told Traci's mom on the phone that before the wedding I would have a job. The only problem is that nothing was coming. I made it a full-time job looking for a full-time job. Application after application, resume after

Claim
your
miracle
now and
wait on
the Lord
to deliver
it.

FROM PRODIGAL TO PRODIGY

resume, interview after interview, nothing was coming through. Like we all do at times when God doesn't show up for us when we think He should, we start poking our lips out and feeling sorry for ourselves. We act like these managers or owners of these companies have power over the God we serve.

I remember one day my mother called me in the middle of my *"pity session."* The weight I was feeling was great and instead of giving it to God, I tried to carry that burden. The stress and burdens that were on my heart soon had me in tears. My mother asked what was wrong. I told her that I was just stressing over a job, but that I knew God was going to handle it. I told her I got my life right; I couldn't see what was taking God so long to bless me. She sternly told me to pick up my head & dry those tears! *"Claim your miracle now and wait on the Lord to deliver it,"* she said. She also told me that it was important that I practice faith and to believe in what I asked for. That message from my mother was right on time!

*"The Lord is disappointed when His people place a low estimate upon themselves. He desires His chosen heritage to value themselves according to the price He has placed upon them. God wanted them, else He would not have sent His Son on such an expensive errand to redeem them. He has a use for them, and He is well pleased when they make the very highest demands upon Him, that they may glorify His name. They may expect large things if they have faith in His promises."* Desire of Ages, p. 668. What Ellen White is saying here is that God expects and wants us to ask for big things from Him. God loves to do for us just as parents find genuine joy in doing things for their children.

I thank God that He doesn't answer all of our prayers. Looking back on life now, if He gave me some things that I asked for when I asked for them, I would have been severely short changing myself. When we live according to God's will for us, we can rest assured that we are in good hands. If God doesn't answer one of our prayers, it's for one of three reasons:

1. He has something better in store for us.
2. He cannot trust us with what we are asking for or it will harm us.
3. He is testing our faith.

God has a funny way of doing things. Isaiah 55:8 says, *"For my thoughts are not your thoughts, neither are your ways my ways, declares the LORD."* NIV. So if God doesn't give you that woman, or man, or house or job, or car that you want, then it might be because He has something better for you. There are some things that God cannot trust us with, so He has to withhold it from us until we are ready. It's not that He doesn't want us to have it, but maybe this thing we want could be the one thing that would keep us from heaven. Until we are spiritually strong enough to have this asset, God will keep it from us.

God will also let us sweat for a little bit. He likes flexing His mighty hand to prove to us over and over again that He is in control. He just wants us to believe in Him. Sometimes when it comes to God working in our lives we get amnesia. We forget that God just opened a door, and we start stressing and doubting His power.

One day a family came home from work and school. As the father placed his brief case on the kitchen table and the mother opened the fridge, their six-year-old daughter sat at the kitchen table. With a loud sigh she put her hands on her head. The parents looked at each other and asked their daughter what was wrong. The daughter said, *"Well the light bill is double this month, and the car note is due this week, and I don't know how I'm going to pay these bills."* The dad replied, *"Why are you stressing over those bills, that's my responsibility!"* Many times we are like that young child worrying about things that we should let our heavenly Father handle. He says to you and me: *"Cast your cares on the LORD and he will sustain you; he will never let the righteous be shaken."* Psalm 55:22, NIV.

Whatever you may have on your load, give it to God. It's time that we treat God like the Great and Mighty God He is! God's word is plain and to the point. In Matthew 7:7, 8, we are admonished to: *"Ask and it will be given to you; seek and you will find; knock and the door will be opened to you. For everyone who asks receives; the one who seeks finds; and to the one who knocks, the door will be opened."* NIV. I think that there is disbelief in the power of God. You may think that for some reason God won't answer your prayers, but you are wrong. The only requirement from God is that you believe in Him that He can grant your request. My suggestion is that you put God to the test. I have, and He has proven faithful to me, every time!

# CHAPTER NINE

## EXCEEDINGLY & ABUNDANTLY

I titled this chapter after the text found in Ephesians 3:20, *"Now unto him that is able to do exceeding abundantly above all that we ask or think, according to the power that worketh in us."* KJV. My journey through life is one that I will never forget. God has spared my life to be a testimony to all. My message is that it's never too late to come home. What's equally important is the fact that when you give God 100% of you and you allow Him to take complete control in your life, the equal reactions are blessings.

One thing that I find interesting as I look back on my life is how God came in and gave me the happiness and structure I so desperately wanted and desired. He just wants us to make Him first in our lives. *"But seek first his kingdom and his righteousness, and all these things will be given to you as well."* Matthew 6:33, NIV. All that God asks from us is that we seek Him first, get to truly know Him, try and love Him like He loves us, and He will give us everything we need. With that said, allow me to share the Reaction to the Action of me giving Jesus my All!

***Blessing #1 - "New Career"***

This is a prime example of God not answering some of our prayers. You see, I was praying for a job. I asked God for a job in the morning, midday, and evening. I just wanted something so that I wasn't sitting at home all day. Then I prayed for a job that would really pay the bills. When nothing came through, I prayed for God's will to be done. I got to the point where I just threw my hands up because I was tired of applying for jobs and getting dressed up for interviews. God said that He wasn't going to give me a job; He wanted to give me a career. When I was unemployed I would sit at home and imagine different salaries and what I could do with them. I never thought I would actually get one of those.

One day I got a call from a guy with this school. The company was looking for a regional recruiter for the state of Alabama. I never even heard of the company, nor did Traci or I apply for the Job. He said that he found my resume and wanted to talk. Not only did I get the job, but it's paying a salary higher that I've ever made, along with health insurance. The job also allows me to work from home, speak, and mentor youth while getting paid to travel. I couldn't imagine such a job, but this is how God operates. He said that since I completely turned my life around He wanted to completely bless me! This new career that the Lord gave me even allows me to enjoy what I'm doing and make a difference in the community.

For the record, I started with the company one and a half months before the wedding; so I fulfilled my promise to Traci and her mom. They were both happy for me. I look back now on how I was rushing God when He just wanted me to sit still and watch Him work. You can imagine how silly I felt asking for those other little jobs that would have made me miserable along with a significantly lower salary.

For so long my actions, thoughts, and feelings placed God in a small box, and at times I doubted that He could work outside of that box.

I think the key for my job breakthrough was praying the right prayer. I was praying for what I wanted in my life. Not only was I settling, but I should have been praying and asking God to give me what He wanted for me to have. God's will for our lives is always better than we can request. This new career was the first of many blessings. Not only was I blessed with my new career, but Traci was given a promotion with her company. To top that of, Traci's company was laying off 30% of their employees but God also saw fit to preserve her job! Praise be to God!

### Blessing # 2 - "I Do!"

Once Traci and I became engaged, we had our hands full of plans for the wedding. We initially planned to have a small wedding but once our mothers got involved our plans changed. I'm still not sure how we pulled off the wedding that we did in four months, but we did. Everything worked out according to God's will. One thing that I think helped out was the fact that we were having our Bible studies, seeking marriage counseling, and practicing abstinence. We were trying to be as obedient as possible. It was not the matter of following God's law; it was more of a love factor. Since we truly loved God, we obeyed His law. You see, when you love someone, you have to put them first. That's what God did; He gave us His son so that we could live. The art of Love is to think of other people.

Too often we as Christians get caught up with God's Law when we should be focusing on God's Love. Many Christians are religious, but rarely relational. While Jesus walked the earth He was very personal and cared for others during His time here. During our engagement process I had to stop thinking about myself and the physical urges I sustained and focused on why I was going through this purification process called abstinence. I told my wife that I was saving myself for her. Once I reached this accomplishment, I knew this wasn't possible without God.

On February 7, 2010, I married my best friend, Traci Shanell Anderson. This was such a great, sacred and blessed day, I'll never forget. I felt so complete being around all of our family and friends, I was delivered from my background of lust and fornication, and could now live with my life partner, experiencing God's grace together.

One great thing about God is that He will find a way to create in your spouse what you want along with what you need. A wise man once suggested to me that God put husbands and wives together to be holy as well as happy. Think about that for a moment. The key elements to a successful marriage are Love, Humility, Communication, Patience, and Trust, which are all characteristics of Christ. He is our Redeemer and most perfect example of true godly love. Most successful marriages are ones where the unconditional love of Christ is practiced without compromise.

### Blessing # 3 - "New Car & Truck"
God decided that He wasn't done blessing us. Our Father is all knowing, all powerful, and never ceases to amaze me. You

see God wants to bless us with things, and He promised in His word that He would supply all our needs. *"And my God will meet all your needs according to the riches of his glory in Christ Jesus"* Philippians 4:19, NIV. In this instance, here Jesus knew that we needed a car. We were sharing Traci's car which was about 10 years old. This car was a blessing to us but with my new job I was required to travel around Alabama and speak at different high schools. This meant that we couldn't share a car, so we needed to get another vehicle.

After several failed attempts, the Lord opened up doors and we were able to get Traci a car, and not just any car, but one of the premier foreign luxury cars. It kind of just fell on our laps, and we were astonished, yet grateful! Now that my new wife has her pretty little car, I was driving the other car for some time now with no complaints. The mileage was pretty high; and I knew that it would be time for a newer vehicle because of the amount of travel I do per week. If it were my choice I would have liked to have a large SUV. That was my style of vehicle. You see when I was managing the car rental company I was accustomed to having a large SUV most of the time. My favorites were the Ford Expeditions, Nissan Armada, and the Yukon Denali or Tahoe. Let me not fail to mention the Infinity QX56!

After running into several issues with finding my vehicle, I just threw my hands up in frustration and said, *"Forget it!"* I told Traci that God Himself was going to have to pick out this car for me. That's where I was in my walk. I wanted God to order all of my steps. I decided that I would drive the old car until it broke down or until God decided to give me another option.

Two days later I got a call from a dealership that I dealt with a few days prior which led to frustration and disappointment. Honestly, when they called me I didn't even want to talk to them, I made up in my mind God would have to send me a car. They called and called and called to tell me about this Ford Expedition that they had and how it was in perfect condition with very little miles. The manager began to tell me how perfect the leather looked and all the details. I continued to decline the offer of even coming to see the truck. After every decline, they would call back every 15 minutes with a new strategy.

By now I'm getting upset thinking to myself what don't they understand about NO? The final call I got was from the general manager, and he assured me that they were working on my behalf, and that if I could stop by one day and just see the truck, he felt I would fall in love with it. I told him that I would talk to my wife and get back to him.

I was sort of impressed on how consistent they were. I left my office after this last phone call with the sales manager and asked my wife what she thought. She told me that it was worth stopping by. I then told her what I decided about having God send me the truck, and she said, *"Don't you think this is what's happening?"* We immediately went to the dealership, and like the manager said, I fell in love with it. The next day I was driving off the lot with my new truck. To God we give the Glory!

I think it's interesting how things came together when I put it in God's hands. There's no telling what was wrong under the hood of those other cars, and being denied was what was protecting me from that. No sooner than two days after putting it all in God's hands, He showed up right on time.

The interesting thing about the situation is I ended up with a large SUV, just like I wanted. *"Take delight in the LORD, and he will give you the desires of your heart."* Psalms 37:4. This makes so much sense, and I experienced it first-hand. God wants to bless us with things; He just wants to make sure that we will love Him with or without that thing we want. Sometimes we make our personal possessions our God and we forget who blessed us with these gifts.

Often times we sit and wish for things, and our not having becomes our focus. We look at what others have and we wonder why we don't have things when we should be thankful for what we do have. We focus so much on the door that was closed that we can't see the door God has opened for us. We must stand still and trust that God will bless us. I know some people who have very little, and they are so in love with God. To see their circumstances and to know there stance on life, it's a blessing to me. I'm reminded of a song by Kirk Franklin, *"I'd rather have Jesus than silver and gold."* There are many blessings that my wife and I have received for which we feel so worthy. Some things God does for us cause me to giggle and say, *"Really God?"* Thanks!

### *Blessing # 4 - "Brand New Home"*

Upon our baptisms, we got married. After the wedding we were both blessed with great careers. After the new careers, the Lord filled the need for new vehicles. Life for us was unbelievably great. All we needed now was a house. We tried to see what our chances were to buy our first home and nothing was working out. My response to our constant house-hunting disappointment was that maybe we are being greedy. I really thought that God had blessed us so much that maybe we should stop asking Him for stuff. Traci felt differently. She told me that God told her we were going to own our own home. She said that she could feel it, and boy was she consistent.

Traci was claiming this house so much that every other day she was bringing home different builders' floor plans and magazines. If she wasn't bringing home floor plans, she would tell me about a new subdivision or she would drag me out to look at the different houses. I would go with the flow of house shopping because I noticed that Traci liked to dream, so I was going to support her dream. Even though I was tired of rejection and knew rejection was around the corner, her faith kept me going on the search for our first home.

Traci and I both were tired of paying rent. We knew that it was cheaper to buy than to just give away money every month. I agreed with her point of view but we didn't really have too many options. House hunting became a sort of a hobby for my wife. This hobby soon paid off. She came home one day excited about a brand new subdivision. She said she was driving home, and she just happened to look up and saw this sign that explained the options of qualifying for a house. She tried her best to explain to me all of the details about being qualified; and she felt that we had a good chance. I figured this was another one of her open house missions requesting my company, so I accepted.

While at this new subdivision, we toured about six brand new model homes and there was one that we fell in love with. The floor plan seemed perfect. So perfect that I was a bit upset that she dragged me here only to be denied once more. After a long talk with the property manager, we realized things were in our favor. A few weeks later, we were paying our deposit, and they were starting on our home.

God loves it when you request big things from Him. Three months later, God blessed my wife and me with a brand new home. Traci was able to pick out everything she wanted in the home from the color of the walls, to the hard wood floors, carpet, cabinets, granite, etc. God is so good! What was now taking place in our lives was God making an example of us. He was putting our lives on a billboard for all the world to see that once you give God your all, that's 100% of yourself to Him, He will bless you abundantly. More than you can even ask or think!

Let's look at this verse again, *"Now to Him who is able to do exceedingly abundantly above all that we ask or think, according to the power that works in us"* Ephesians 3:20, KJV. The power that works in us is the power we receive from God. The verse here says that God can bless you in ways that you couldn't even think or ask for. There were things that God blessed me with that I would have never thought would happen. Many times we expect too less from God. We must realize that the cattle on a thousand hills belong to our God. Don't you know that our God is the ruler of all the worlds and galaxies? Our planet is but a spec to His marvelous creations, and He finds joy in blessing us.

Let's take another look at what took place with the Prodigal son once he came home to his father in repentance. Luke 15:20-24, NIV, says: *"So he got up and went to his father. But while he was still a long way off, his father saw him and was filled with compassion for him; he ran to his son, threw his arms around him and kissed him. The son said to him, 'Father, I have sinned against heaven and against you. I am no longer worthy to be called your son.' "But the father said to his servants, 'Quick!*

*Bring the best robe and put it on him. Put a ring on his finger and sandals on his feet. Bring the fattened calf and kill it. Let's have a feast and celebrate. For this son of mine was dead and is alive again; he was lost and is found.' So they began to celebrate."* The same thing takes place when we come back to God. The Bible says that all of heaven rejoices once a sinner is reborn again. Don't take my word for it; it's in God's Holy Word: *"I tell you that in the same way there will be more rejoicing in heaven over one sinner who repents than over ninety-nine righteous persons who do not need to repent."* Luke 15:7, NIV.

What a great Love this is that God has for us. I guess that's because God IS Love! I am a living witness that like the father did in the parable of the prodigal son, our heavenly Father does for us. In spite of my wicked past, He still loved me and accepted me with open arms! God finds joy in blessing us. All we must do is delight ourselves in Him, and His will, yes, and He will give us all of the things we desire. The same way a parent finds joy in seeing their son or daughter open a birthday gift or a Christmas gift, is the same type of feeling our God feels about blessing us. Your heavenly father rejoices when His lost children find their way home. God wants, will, and can restore your life.

# CHAPTER TEN

## GPS

### *"Seven Tips to staying on course."*

Life is like taking a road trip filled with traffic, detours, roadblocks, and short cuts. In every trip we take there is a specific destination that we seek. We all have a destination we are ultimately going to; so let's look at our life in that same context. We are either going down the road of death and destruction, or we are traveling up the highway to heaven.

Many times we get off track or turned around on the way. Sometimes like I've experienced, you'll think you're going in the right direction only to find out you are lost. Some of us are lost and don't know we are lost; and once we realize that we are lost, we think that we are too far off course to turn back.

If this is how you feel today, I'm here to tell you that it's not too late to make a life-changing U-turn. All we have to do is get back on track and stay our course. We must plug in our own GPS *"God's Positioning System,"* and use it to navigate your way back home. We must position ourselves in the direction of God! Just like a GPS, we tend to question the route it's taking us; but just like we trust the man-made GPS, we are to trust our Father's *"GPS"*.

### Tip # 1 - Believe

As you take this journey of reforming your life, there are several things that you must believe in. The first is the belief and recognition that there are some things in your life that you need to change. There is sin in all of our lives. Your sins may not be what mine were. Maybe you're dealing with greed, homosexuality, lying, hate, but whatever it is, that sin must be identified.

Once we have identified the sins in our life, we must realize that change is necessary. I once heard a pastor say that change is a characteristic of a Christian. In order to be comfortable with God, we must be comfortable with change. If you feel you can't be changed, you're wrong! Jesus looked at them and said, *"With man this is impossible, but with God all things are possible."* Matthew 19:26, NIV. Once we confess our sins to God, He has the power to change us. The Holy Spirit is the one who does the conversion within our hearts.

The devil's biggest lie that he told me most of the time was, *"You can't change!"* Has he told you that lie too? Do you think that you've done so much wrong, that God doesn't love you, and he can't forgive you? Let me remind you that Satan is the master deceiver. *"For God so loved the world that he gave his one and only Son, that whoever believes in him shall not perish but have eternal life."* John 3:16, NIV. Salvation was paid on Calvary over 2000 years ago and is free for you and me, if we accept it!

The same way Satan told Adam and Eve in the garden that they wouldn't surely die, he is telling us that everything is going to be alright, and that there shouldn't be any urgency to getting your life together. We must claim the victory over Satan; but in order to do this, you must believe in the power of God and the Blood that was shed.

We must realize that we need victory over the sins in our lives, and that God has already forgiven us because He died for those sins and through His blood that was shed on Calvary, Salvation is ours. It's important that we believe that through Christ Jesus we can change and have the victory over the enemy! *"Therefore, if anyone is in Christ, he is a new creation; the old has gone, the new is here!"* 2 Corinthians 5:17, NIV. This scripture is telling us that we can be changed and be new creatures in Christ. You can never go too far beyond God's grace.

There were two prayers that I had to pray when it came to me and my problems with sin. Before I prayed for the power to change, I had to pray for the will and desire to change. Think about this for a minute. Many times we ask for the power do to something we really don't want to do. My prayer went like this, *"Lord I know the sins that I commit everyday hurt You. I enjoy this sin, and I don't want to stop. I realize that I cannot continue to sin and still receive the salvation that is waiting on me; so I'm asking that You give me the desire to do Your will."*

Now once you've prayed this prayer and God has given you the will to do His will, you can now ask for the power. Once God has given you His power, you can expect the victory because God is Victorious! A praying sinner is stronger than the enemy and his demons!

### Tip # 2 - *"Assist the Holy Spirit"*
The Holy Spirit wants to do great things in our soul, but we

There are over 75 different verses in the Bible that give warnings of the negative effects of alcohol.

must give Him the opportunity to work. In order for the Holy Spirit to work fully in our hearts, we must be receptive to its voice. This, at times, may be a struggle and we set ourselves at a disadvantage because our minds are cloudy. *"Do you not know that your bodies are temples of the Holy Spirit, who is in you, whom you have received from God? You are not your own; you were bought at a price. Therefore honor God with your bodies."* 1 Corinthians 6:19, 20, NIV.

This scripture is telling us plainly that our bodies naturally come with the dwelling of the Holy Spirit. Many of the pollutants we put in our bodies cloud our thinking and affect our actions. I have experienced these pollutants firsthand. The devil packages it up in a hip, pretty package with bows and sweet smelling scents. We must be cautious of these highly deceiving pollutants such as Alcohol, Drugs, Tobacco, Pornography, Secular Music, etc. I know these seem great and, like I once did, you probably enjoy partaking in these things; but trust me, they only leave you addicted and empty.

Alcohol is an intoxicant that I struggled with for years. This liquid drug goes straight to your blood stream, which ultimately affects the brain and how you think. Think about it, once you drink, you become loose. The more you drink, the more you tap into your subconscious state of mind. When you are not under the influence, you are able to think, make rational, decisions, and commune clearly with the Holy Spirit. We are naturally prone to sin, which is why our subconscious thinking is so raw at times. *"Wine is a mocker, strong drink is raging: and whosoever is deceived thereby is not wise."* Proverbs 20:1, KJV.

There are over 75 different verses in the Bible that give

warnings of the negative effects of alcohol. There are those who will try and justify drinking by saying it's OK as long as they don't get drunk; so let me say this. Let's look at 1 Peter 5:8, NIV, *"Be alert and of sober mind. Your enemy the devil prowls around like a roaring lion looking for someone to devour."* This text is quite simple. Be sober, stay away from hard drinks. Satan has been deceiving us from the beginning. He is the master deceiver; he was able to deceive one-third of the Angels in Heaven!

Sin starts in the mind, so why would you want to put something in your body that would alter your thinking and block you from hearing the voice of the Holy Spirit. I would often tell myself that I was a casual drinker and that there was nothing wrong with it. I realize now that alcohol has no part in the Body of Christ. God wants to dwell within your body, and in order for Him to do the work He wants to do within you, there must be a complete surrender. You must give Him a clear temple in which to dwell.

Tobacco can have the same affect or worse on your body and your spirit. It is known for frying your nerves and making you addicted and dependent on it. God wants His children free from this. I was once addicted to cigarettes and Black & Mild's. Tobacco is known to give you a temporary fix, but causes serious respiratory problems, bad breath, and gum disease. God doesn't want this for His people. If you truly want to be set free from tobacco, you must fully rely on God to help you. I know that it can be done because He did it for me; and He can do it for you. After that evening in my garage, I haven't picked up any form of tobacco. I praise God for delivering me from this killer.

There are several different drugs that are strategically

We
cannot
fight this
battle
ourselves.
We need
the Spirit
of God.

placed all over earth by Satan himself. Some of these drugs are made in a lab with numerous life-threatening chemicals, some of which come from right here on earth. I once told my dad that marijuana grew from the earth, and that it must be from God. His response was, *"So does poison Ivy; why don't you try putting that to your lips and see how good you feel."* That statement of course made me think!

Many times in life we focus so much on things to make us feel good; as Christ did, it's important that we as Christians practice temperance in all things. Society today is so fixed on pleasing ourselves; no one wants to please God. Ellen G. White, in her book, *"Confrontation,"* states, *"How we are victims of a depraved appetite, goaded by Satan's continual temptations we seek indulgence at the expense of health and even life."* In the act of chasing the feeling of relief or pleasure we are killing the very bodies we are trying to please. Wow!

Drugs possess our minds and allow for demons to enter and control our thoughts and bodies. I have been possessed many times before by becoming drunk and high; and throughout the night I would move about the city only to ask the next day what took place. Even if I did remember what happened whenever I was intoxicated, I was always acting out of character or doing things I wouldn't normally do.

Think about this for a moment; if we don't give the Holy Spirit full control, then to whom do we give the power over our bodies and mind? If you're drunk or high on drugs, you have opened the door to be controlled by someone or something other than God. *"For we are not fighting against flesh and blood enemies, but against evil rulers and authorities of the unseen world, against mighty powers in this dark world, and against evil spirits in the heavenly places."* Ephesians 6:12, NLT. Just because we can't see the battle going on for our souls, doesn't mean it's not taking place. Ephesians tells us here that we are battling spiritual forces. We cannot fight this battle ourselves. We need the Spirit of God.

This is why it is so important that we keep our bodies, minds, and souls clear of drugs and other intoxicants. When we partake in these substances, we give the enemy the advantage over our lives. In order for us to truly walk in God's light and to allow the Holy Spirit to lead our actions and thoughts, we must keep our minds clear so that we can get clear directions from Him.

Music has more power over our minds and thoughts than we want to think or believe. Think about this for a second; music naturally affects our moods. Classical or soft music tends to calm us down; while rock, rap or heavy metal music tend to drive, excite or pump us up emotionally and physically. There are countless articles and books that discuss the physical, mental, and emotional effects of music.

The concern with music is not necessarily the beat but more with the message and lyrics. The lyrics that we listen to mold our character and thought process. It's important that the music we listen to supports the lifestyle that we want to live. One thing that helped me out was my lack of rap music. The message from the music I listened to promoted the opposite lifestyle I wanted. For others it may be a different type of music, but I found that when I was listening to certain songs or music, it put me in specific mood. When I listened to sexually explicit songs, it would put me in the mood for sexual fulfillment. You may say that music doesn't make you think or do anything, but

Prayer is
our direct
line to our
Father in
heaven.

FROM PRODIGAL TO PRODIGY

whatever your conscious doesn't pick up, your subconscious will. It is important that we feed our minds with music that will nurture our souls and promote a positive thought process.

### Tip # 3 - "Prayer & Devotion

Daily prayer and devotion are the two fundamental things to having and keeping a real relationship with God. Prayer is our direct line to our Father in heaven. When we have our daily devotion and Bible study, we grow spiritually. This is a time when we can learn more about God and His plan for us. In order for any relationship to grow, you need time and communication.

Prayer does many things for you. The Seventh-Day Adventist Encyclopedia Commentary reference series, page 376, says this about prayer: *"Prayer is the breath of the soul,(GW 254) and is essential to spiritual life as breath is to physical health. Neglect of prayer results in spiritual anemia. Those who come to God must do so with a sincere heart."*

Prayer also helps you know God better; this is your connection to Him. You also receive power from prayer as well as deliverance from sin and temptation. Even Jesus needed prayer, and warned his disciples of this. *"On reaching the place, he said to them, 'Pray that you will not fall into temptation"* Luke 22:40, NIV. There was a time when Jesus asked His disciples to pray for Him for He knew the power of prayer.

Daily devotion and Bible study are ways that we can stay in tune with God's will. We find encouragement from the Word of God. *"All Scripture is God-breathed and is useful for teaching, rebuking, correcting and training in righteousness."* 2 Timothy 3:16, NIV. God's word is here for us; and this is what the enemy of God and his kingdom don't want you reading.

There is a story in the Bible for every single situation that life has to offer. The closer you get in the Word of God, the closer you get to know God. When it comes to reading the Bible, start off small with a couple of verses, and then work your way up to a chapter. We all need constant communion with God's Word, and I suggest that you start and end your day with God.

There are times when we are so consumed mentally from television and movies and other things that keep our brains moving fast, that when we crack open our Bible or hear a word from God, we get sleepy because we're not being stimulated at a high frequency. The devil wants you to feel that God's Word and other Bible-based devotionals are boring; or he will try his best to keep you busy with other things that have the opposite effect on your soul salvation.

Finding some quiet time daily with God will work wonders! Prayer and devotion will assist you with hearing and knowing God on a real personal level. Just like any relationship, it takes time to build. Don't be afraid to ask God what you want or need. *"So I say to you: Ask and it will be given to you; seek and you will find; knock and the door will be opened to you."* Luke 11:9, NIV.

### Tip # 4 - *"Spiritual Support"*

We all know that there is strength in numbers. Once you have decided to give your life to God and you have a desire to make a life-changing U-turn, it's imperative that you surround yourself with people who will support your new lifestyle. There's nothing like the encouragement you will receive from

Even
the most
powerful
God-
centered
men and
women in
the Bible
needed
spiritual
help and
support.

a fellow Christian brother or sister. *"Two are better than one, because they have a good return for their labor: If either of them falls down, one can help the other up. But pity anyone who falls and has no one to help them up."* Ecclesiastes 4:9, 10, NIV. Even Jesus had support. As a matter of fact, Christ had 12 disciples that were with him constantly. Christian fellowship is critical, especially during these last days.

I am reminded of a story that took place in Exodus 17. Joshua is leading Israel to battle with the Amalekites. While Israel is in battle, Moses is at the top of the hill, and he has his hands lifted to God above. As long as his hands where lifted to God, Israel prevailed. When Moses' hands got tired and fell, the Amalekites would get the advantage. As Moses' hands were heavy, Aaron and Hur took stones and placed them under Moses' hand and sat there, each of them holding up one arm. They held up Moses' arms until the sun set and Israel won the battle.

I find this story to be very symbolic. When we are in life's spiritual battles it's important that we keep our hands lifted to God for that's where our power comes from. What I also find significant about this story is the help that Moses needed. Even the most powerful God-centered men and women in the Bible needed spiritual help and support.

Someone of spiritual support is someone who will not only pray with you, but will pray for you. *"Confess your sins to each other and pray for each other so that you may be healed. The earnest prayer of a righteous person has great power and produces wonderful results."* James 5:16, NLT. Prayer partners are a great fellowship as well; they will give you support and encouragement. It's also good to have someone in your life with whom you can share testimonies and discuss the goodness of God while studying the Word. *"And they overcame him by the blood of the Lamb, and by the word of their testimony; and they loved not their lives unto the death."* Rev 12:11, KJV. God will turn your Test into a Testimony. You are to share your testimony so that you can declare the goodness of God, as well as motivate and encourage others. You don't have to worry about finding people who will be spiritually supportive because God will send them your way.

### Tip # 5 - *"Successful Positions"*

Placing yourself in a position to be successful is important. In order to get the victory over sin, you must refrain from sinful endeavors. Watch the environment you're in and the company you keep. Just the same as finding positive people to fellowship with, you want to also cut off communication with those who have a negative influence on you. Now, I'm not telling you to abandon your friends. That's not what Christ did at all; but if you have a problem with lust or pornography, and your friends are going to the strip club, then you should probably sit that trip out.

Just the same way alcoholics should stay away from bars; you should watch the places you dwell. After you grow in Christ, you may be able to go certain places without relapsing; but while you are still fresh in your walk, it is best that you stay clear of any diversions. The enemy is cunning and wise; and he will use whatever he can to get you back on the road of destruction and death. I think about the first time humans fell to the temptations of sin. *"And when the woman saw that the tree was good for food, and that it was pleasant to the eyes, and a*

The enemy will tempt you when you're alone and in a vulnerable state.

FROM PRODIGAL TO PRODIGY

*tree to be desired to make one wise, she took of the fruit thereof, and did eat, and gave also unto her husband with her; and he did eat."* Genesis 3:6, KJV. It was when Eve met the serpent near the tree of knowledge of good and evil that she was deceived.

Being near the forbidden tree is when she came across the serpent. She was able to see the serpent eat the fruit and not die, which I'm sure helped his case. I can just imagine the serpent was overly expressing how good and extra juicy the fruit was, making Eve feel like she was missing out. Eve did not realize that the effects of her disobedience and self-pleasing would cost humanity for generations to come.

If Eve had been near her husband, Adam, she probably wouldn't have given in. This proves the last point that there is strength in numbers. The enemy will tempt you when you're alone and in a vulnerable state. The enemy will make his sin taste as sweet as fruit only to find out that the sweet pleasure is sin. Placing yourself in nurturing environments that will support your new journey with God is another key to successful living on your journey to salvation.

### Tip # 6 - "Service"

Service is a well-known characteristic of Christians. Jesus was sent here to earth to be our Redeemer, and to set the perfect example for us by living a life of service. The King of Kings, the Prince of Peace while here on earth served others everyday; then ultimately gave His life for us all. Jesus lived a life of ministry and service, often times just meeting the physical needs of people.

Love is the act of thinking of others or putting someone else before you. I have often heard that God does not love,

God is Love! Christian service and ministry are key to keeping the flame and burning desire of Christ in your life. It's an opportunity to reach out to others and show the love of God. This was one thing that really sustained me when I came back to the church. I remember Momma Pat Simmonds kept me on the track of service and would not let me slip. She knew the importance of constant service and ministry for God's people.

It's time for us to claim this inner Prodigy that we have and be the true salt of the world. *"You are the salt of the earth, but if salt has lost its taste, how shall its saltiness be restored? It is no longer good for anything except to be thrown out and trampled under people's feet. You are the light of the world. A city set on a hill cannot be hidden."* Matthew 5:13, 14, ESV. You see here that God wants us to be the salt of the earth adding His flavor upon this land, as well as a beacon of light for all to see. God's light should radiate through us all.

Service and ministry also keep you humble and active. *"What does it profit, my brethren, if someone says he has faith but does not have works? Can faith save him?"* James 2:14, NKJV. Here the Bible is saying that Faith without Works is dead. You must have works. God has called all Christians to be fishers of men.

Once we truly realize our potential and strength we have in God, we can wage war against the enemy. Every true Christian will have a true desire to help others and share with them the goodness of the Lord. Everyone doesn't need to be a preacher. God has given us all specific gifts of service; He's just waiting on us to use them to His glory.

God "dwells" in
the atmosphere
of His praise.

FROM PRODIGAL TO PRODIGY

### *Tip # 7 – "Unconditional Praise"*

In Psalms 22:3, the Bible says that God inhabits the praises of His people. In other words, God *"dwells"* in the atmosphere of His praise. This means that praise is not a reaction that we get from being in God's presence, but praise is actually an act of faith which brings us into the presence and power of God!

There are all sorts of actions you can participate in praising God. Some may give verbal thanks or expressions of adoration and thanksgiving. Some may sing or play instruments. Others may shout, dance, or clap their hands. It is important that we practice true praise, and not just go through the motions. Jesus spoke of the hypocrisy of the Pharisees. Their worship was an outward show and not truly from the heart. *"These people honor me with their lips, but their hearts are far from me."* Matthew 15:8, NIV). When you give genuine praise to God, it should be a matter of humility and sincere devotion to the Lord from within.

It's important that you give thanks and praise to God even when things aren't perfect. Far too often, we only want to give God His praise when He works a miracle. We need to learn to worship and be thankful to God regardless of our situation.

Many times you will receive your breakthrough or Blessing after you give thanks to God. *"Enter his gates with thanksgiving and his courts with praise; give thanks to him and praise his name. For the LORD is good and his love endures forever; his faithfulness continues through all generations."* Psalm 100:4, 5, NIV. Once you really understand this verse, you can't help but give God all of the Glory and Honor! Praise is also a way to say *"Thank You"* to God for where he has bought you in your life.

Worship confuses the enemy especially when things are

not going the way you think they should. The safest place in the world is in the will of God! So when that storm comes, embrace the rain. Like the trees in the ground, you cannot grow without rain. Rest assured that God will never give you more than you can handle. I'm sure you've heard this quote before, *"What doesn't kill you makes you stronger!"* Well look at your spiritual life the same way. Every challenge or obstacle that God allows to come your way only makes you stronger within Him; so thank God for the spiritual strength training!

# FINAL WORD

My life is a living testimony, and proof that God restores. The purpose for this book is to encourage you that it's never too late to give God your all. We all fall short from the glory of God, but praise God for grace and mercy! Whether you consider your sins big or small, confess them to God and receive the full strength of the Holy Spirit. Let me share with you my favorite verse in the Bible:

*"If my people, who are called by my name, will humble themselves and pray and seek my face and turn from their wicked ways, then will I hear from heaven and will forgive their sin and will heal their land."* 2 Chronicles 7:14.

In this verse here God is claiming us in spite of our mess. He says *"If My People!"* Then He confirms that we are called by His name meaning *"Child of God"* and ask that we Humble ourselves *"admit that were in sin."* God also requests that we pray to Him, *"recognize only He can set us free"* then Seek His face, *"look unto Him,"* and turn from our wicked ways *"repent for our sins."* God then says that He will hear from Heaven, forgive our sins and heal our land. This is where Restoration takes place. If you want to be made new and have your life restored, follow this formula.

It is not too late to make a life changing U-turn. Please

It is
not too late
to make a
life changing
U-Turn.

adhere to my testimony and warning. God spared my life from my wicked and wasteful lifestyle so that I could warn you. Take it from someone who has been lost and has now found his way home. God wants prosperity for you! Satan wants to destroy you!

God wants you to live with Him forever! Satan wants you to burn with him. God can give you an indescribable joy! Satan can only give you temporary happiness. God is just and true! Satan is a liar!

The world that we live in will come to an end sooner than we think. God still has a great work for us to do! The price for salvation has already been paid. God has created you for a reason. John 14:12 says: *"I tell you the truth, anyone who believes in me will do the same works I have done, and even greater works, because I am going to be with the Father."* NLT. Did you read that? Jesus clearly states that if we have faith in God, He will give us the power to do greater things than He did while here on Earth.

It is my deepest prayer that you have been encouraged to know that you can never go so far that God cannot reach you. Please don't use my story as a reason to fall victim to sin on purpose knowing that God will save you! Not everyone is as fortunate as I was. I have friends who are dead or are in prison as well as friends who are preachers and doctors. God has given us all the power of choice; I pray that you choose God. It is time to put aside our Prodigal ways and claim the inner Prodigy in all of us! God has a wonderful plan for your life; but you've got to surrender completely to Him and trust Him to work out His plan for you. Jeremiah 29:11 says, *"For I know the plans I have for you,"* declares the LORD, *plans to prosper you and not to harm you, plans to give you hope and a future."* NIV.

God is calling you. Will you answer His call?

# NOTES

1. The Merriam-Webster Dictionary, by Merriam-Webster, Inc 7-28-2004.

2. The Desire of Ages, Ellen G. White, Pacific Press Publishing Association 2005.

3. The Holy Bible, New International Version®, NIV® Copyright © 1973, 1978, 1984, 2011 by Biblica, Inc.™ Used by permission. All rights reserved worldwide.

4. The Holy Bible, New King James Version. Copyright © 1982 by Thomas Nelson, Inc. Used by permission. All rights reserved.

5. The Holy Bible, King James Version present on the Bible Gateway matches the 1987 printing. The KJV is public domain in the United States.

6. New Living Translation, copyright © 1996, 2004, 2007 by Tyndale House Foundation. Used by permission of Tyndale House Publishers, Inc., Carol Stream, Illinois 60188. All rights reserved.

7. The Holy Bible, English Standard Version (ESV) is adapted from the Revised Standard Version of the Bible, Copyright Division of Christian Education of the National Council of the Churches of Christ in the U.S.A. All rights reserved.

8. The Seventh-Day Adventist Encyclopedia Commentary reference series, page 376, copyright 1996 by Review & Herald Publishing Association.

9. Maya Angelou. "A woman's heart should be so hidden in God that a man has to seek Him just to find her," is quoted from her poem "Christians."

SPIRIT REIGN
c o m m u n i c a t i o n s

- Public Speaker

- Mentor

- Youth Counselor

## Book Jeremy Anderson for your next event!

Need a speaker who will Educate, Enlighten & Encourage your Church, Organization, Youth, or Group?
Jeremy's has made ministry his life by traveling and speaking. His passion is reaching out to others from all walks of life to help them find their inner Prodigy.

For booking or more information, contact:
256-759-7492 * Prodigal2Prodigy@gmail.com
29806 Park Hill Dr. Madison, AL
www.spiritreign.org

the
PRODIGAL2PRODIGY
p r o j e c t

# SPIRIT REIGN
## communications

I am overwhelmed with joy to share this pivotal moment with my son Jeremy J. Anderson. It has been an honor and a blessing raising him along side my lovely wife Tawanna. For me, this book is further affirmation of what I've believed for many years. God has placed a call on Jeremy's life that is now coming to fruition as he orders his steps in the way of the Lord. Proverbs 22: 6 say, *"Train up a child in the way he should go: and when he is old, he will not depart from it."* Jeremy's testimony is proof that this biblical formula for success works. The text is not saying that our children will not make mistakes born out of foolish decisions in life. It is saying that when we as parents raise our children with godly admonition as their guide, we are giving them something to fall back on, as was in the case with the prodigal son. If a young person doesn't have the foundation of Christ-centered common sense etched in their memory, they will have nothing to cushion them when or if they fall when they need it the most. The greatest favor or gift we can give our children is a knowledge of Jesus Christ. I thank God everyday for the payoff of the prayers that have gone up for my children throughout the course of their lives.

Daryl S. Anderson Sr.
Founder / CEO
Spirit Reign Communications &
Publishing

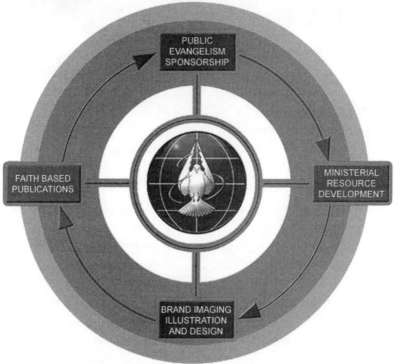

Spirit Reign Communications is a faith based organization dedicated to the development and distribution of ministerial resource materials that effectively communicate the word of God in the 21st century. Our products range from published works to multi-media productions with innovative contemporary slants on the age old gospel message. We partnership with ministries that concur with our doctrinal beliefs of obedience to God, faith in Jesus Christ, and the plan of salvation. We are proud sponsors of "Families At The Alter Ministries" founded by Pastor / Evangelist Daryl S. Anderson Sr.

In our commitment to excellence, we take serving the needs of our customers very serious as we help you meet the needs of your constituents through our vast array of goods and services. We also provide fund-raising incentive packets designed especially for schools, churches, and spiritually based non-profit organizations. Along with our brand of published resource materials we offer professional art and design services for promoting or creating individual corporate identity of Christ-centered institutions.

Spirit Reign offers opportunities for independent sales representatives looking for full-time or part-time employment.

# SPIRIT REIGN
## communications

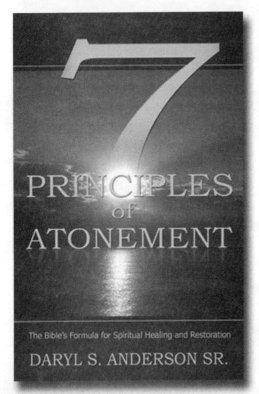

7
PRINCIPLES
of
ATONEMENT

The Bible's Formula for Spiritual Healing and Restoration

DARYL S. ANDERSON SR.

1. *LOVE:* If my people, which are called by my name,

2. *HUMILITY:* shall humble themselves,

3. *FAITH:* and pray,

4. *OBEDIENCE:* and seek my face,

5. *REPENTANCE:* and turn from their wicked ways;

6. *FORGIVENESS:* then will I hear from heaven, and will for give their sin.

7. *RESTORATION:* and will heal their land.

# AVAILABLE IN MAY 2011

The Bible is a book full of formulas created by God to work in behalf of his people. The word Atonement, which means at-one-meant or what it means to be at one with God is what every person should strive to achieve. This book contains Seven important rules of life that are the ingredients in a formula made by God to yield successful results for those who live by them with a pure and earnest heart. The outcome of this biblical remedy is healing and restoration in all areas of life according to the word of God. The Seven Principles of Atonement is based on the covenant promise found in 2 Chronicles 7: 14.